Bad Doctors

Military Justice Proceedings
Against 622 Civil War Surgeons

Thomas P. Lowry

and

Terry Reimer

Cover photo: Dr. David G. Rush
Courtesy of the Library of Congress
LC-B813-2244C.

Copyright © 2010 National Museum of Civil War Medicine

www.civilwarmed.org

Produced with the support of the NMCWM Press

ISBN 1453810854

ISBN 9781453810859

Contents

Acknowledgements	v
Introduction	vii
Chapter 1	
The Roster	1
Chapter 2	
Special Cases	73
Chapter 3	
United States Navy Surgeons	95
Chapter 4	
Confederate Surgeons	99
Chapter 5	
Conclusions	105
Appendices	109
Index	121

Acknowledgements

The National Museum of Civil War Medicine has, for decades, been a place of encouragement for scholars and a repository of knowledge for the public, for everything related to mid-Victorian medicine. Of especial help in the preparation of this book have been Andrew Hamilton and Barry Thompson. Their long hours in the museum and at the National Archives have been of vital assistance.

At the Iowa Board of Medicine, Amy Van Maanen, Director of Licensure and Administration, was generous with her time, in providing present day data on medical misbehavior.

In regard to doctors removed by "direct dismissal" rather than by court-martial we owe much to Valerie Josephson, who provided us with a complete set of the *United States Service Magazine.* Jack D. Welsh, retired professor of medicine and gastroenterology, and prolific researcher, was instrumental in the preparation of *Tarnished Scalpels,* the first major study of Civil War medical malfeasance. The Rev. A. H. Ledoux was both helpful and resourceful in tracing the families and post-war careers of these doctors. F. Terry Hambrecht was endlessly helpful with Confederate doctors.

The massive survey of all Civil War courts-martial, under the aegis of The Index Project, was launched by Robert K. Krick and Michael P. Musick, and conducted by Beverly A. Lowry with the assistance of Thomas P. Lowry. James I. Robertson, Jr. and William C. Davis encouraged and publicized our initial foray into the less heroic aspects of the war. Vonnie Zullo answered many urgent calls for some missing snippet, findable only in the National Archives. To all those we may have overlooked we offer our apologies and our thanks.

Terry Reimer   Thomas P. Lowry

Introduction

As in most circumstances, Civil War soldiers were exposed to all types of surgeons—covering the spectrum from the good to the bad. It must be remembered that physicians did not hold an exalted place in society in the nineteenth century. Quacks and snake-oil salesmen influenced the public's attitudes on medicine, and even some of the mainstream medical practices had a negative effect on public opinion. All physicians were referred to as surgeons, whether they studied surgical procedures or not. Many soldiers were wary of the army surgeons, often preferring to self-medicate rather than risk their lives and health to what they perceived as incompetent physicians. Not everyone felt this way, but the undercurrent of suspicion was definitely present.

In the 1860s medicine was just emerging from the "heroic era," with its theory of bringing a balance to the humors of the body. Bleeding, cupping and purging were still used to treat patients, but these practices were beginning to be replaced by medicines and treatments less dependent on the old theories. Medical practitioners did not know the exact cause of many diseases or the mechanisms of infection, but they were beginning to understand the benefits that cleanliness and good sanitation had in preventing disease and in aiding the healing process. They had no knowledge of germ theory or antiseptic practices, since both discoveries were still years away.

Medical Education

Medical training in the mid-nineteenth century was very different from modern medical education. There was no national organized system of licensing, nor was there a requirement that the person calling themselves a physician had attended medical school. In the early days in America, medical education consisted of an apprenticeship with a practicing physician. Medical schools were established to provide organized lectures to supplement the practical learning of an apprenticeship. The first school, the Philadelphia College of Medicine (now the University of Pennsylvania), opened in 1765. There were no education requirements for admittance into medical school. In the early nineteenth century, at least 80 percent of all doctors entered practice after having served only an apprenticeship. By the start of the Civil War the statistics were reversed--80 percent of practitioners were medical school graduates.

By 1860 a total of one hundred medical schools had opened, although many were only open for a few years, so that by early 1861 there were sixty-four medical schools operating in the United States. There were forty-eight "regular," or allopathic, schools and sixteen schools operated by one or another of the sectarian groups. Two of these schools were for women only. Twenty-four of the medical schools were in the South (defined here as being south of the Mason-Dixon Line). Of the sixteen schools located in states that subsequently seceded from the Union, only the Medical College of Virginia and the University of Virginia remained open during the war.

The majority of medical schools were owned by the teaching faculty who were paid directly by the students through the sale of tickets to the lectures. The usual course of study in a medical school consisted of two terms of six-month-long lectures, with the second term often being a repeat of the first. There was little or no clinical experience, and contact with actual patients was very limited or nonexistent. Most graduates had little opportunity to practice surgical procedures.

Doctors who served with the armies of both the North and the South were often classmates, often from the larger schools in the northern cities. As such, they not only had a shared knowledge, but many also had personal friendships which helped bridge the divide during the war.

Sectarian Medicine

We tend to think of the medical establishment as a monolithic entity, with a shared view and single set of beliefs. That is not the case today, nor was it the case during the Civil War. The nineteenth century saw the development of a number of alternative medical sects which separated themselves from mainstream allopathic medicine. The harsh treatments of the "heroic era" of medicine caused a backlash in the population and led to the rise of the dissident groups. These medical

Introduction

practitioners wished to eliminate bloodletting and the use of harsh drugs containing mercury and other dangerous substances.

The different sects began to emerge in the early 1800s. Thomsonian medicine was established by an herbalist, Samuel Thomson, and his new approach to treating disease was with basic herbal medicines. Over time, Thompsonian medicine evolved into what was called botanic medicine, then into reformed medicine and eventually into eclectic medicine. Samuel Hahnemann, a conventionally-trained physician, founded homeopathy in Germany in the early 1800s. Homeopathy is the use of small amounts of drugs to cause symptoms similar to the disease in a healthy person. These two groups, plus other smaller sects, made inroads into the practice of medicine in America. Some sects even opened medical schools to promote their practices.

The response of organized medicine was, of course, to deny the legitimacy of these dissenting sects. The American Medical Association went so far as to pass a resolution opposing homeopathy in 1855. By the time of the Civil War, the principle medical divisions were allopathy (conventional medicine), homeopathy, and eclectic medicine. The last two sects accounted for more than ten percent of all practicing physicians in 1860. It must be stated that many of the allopathic physicians were also opposed to some of the harsh treatments and medicines, so the lines of demarcation were beginning to blur. Nevertheless, the Union Army was opposed to commissioning physicians who admitted to practicing homeopathy, eclecticism, or any of the other types of sectarian medicine. Many were prevented from serving unless they hid their true leanings concerning medical practices. The establishment doctors went so far as to call the sectarian practitioners "Irregulars."

Quantity

The pre-war Medical Corps of the United States Army consisted of one surgeon general, thirty surgeons, and eighty-four assistant surgeons. Of these surgeons, twenty-four resigned their commissions to serve the Confederacy. The Medical Departments on both sides of the conflict had to expand quickly to meet the demands of war. On the Union side, the hierarchy consisted of: surgeon general, assistant surgeon general, medical inspector general, medical inspectors, medical purveyors, regular army surgeons and assistant surgeons, brigade surgeons (also called surgeons of volunteers), regimental surgeons and assistant surgeons, acting assistant surgeons, medical cadets and hospital stewards. The Confederate Medical Department had a similar hierarchy.

The surgeon general had overall control of the Medical Department and reported to the secretary of war. The medical inspector general and the medical inspectors were responsible for the sanitary conditions of the army in the field, on the transports, and in the hospitals. The medical purveyors were in charge of the selection and purchase of the medical supplies, drugs, instruments, equipment and furniture needed by the Medical Department.

The regular army surgeons and assistant surgeons were the senior staff physicians. The brigade surgeons were volunteers who were attached to the Medical Staff rather than to a specific regiment. They reported directly to the surgeon general, and by 1862 had become the equals of the regular army surgeons. Both of these groups could be called on to perform the duties of medical directors of armies, corps, or divisions in the field, or to be in charge of specific hospitals.

The regimental surgeons were commissioned by the individual states and were permanently attached to their regiments. Occasionally they would be detached for special duty, usually in one of the permanent hospitals. Acting assistant surgeons, also called contract surgeons, were physicians who served under contract with the army. They were not commissioned and were considered private citizens. They mainly served in the hospitals, but also served with regiments in the field and in the aftermath of battles. Medical cadets were usually young medical students who served as hospital assistants. Hospital stewards were non-commissioned officers who performed the duties of druggists, clerks, and storekeepers.

By the end of the war, the number of Union surgeons who served included 170 regular army surgeons and assistant surgeons, 547 surgeons and assistant surgeons of volunteers, 2,109 regimental surgeons, 3,882 regimental assistant surgeons, 85 acting staff surgeons and at least 5,532 acting assistant surgeons. The number of medical cadets and the number of hospital stewards is not known.

Introduction

In all, over 12,000 physicians served the Union in some capacity, either in regiments, on ships, or as surgeons in the many hospitals. An estimated 8,000 physicians served for the Confederacy; of these, approximately 6,800 were appointed, while at least 1,200 served as contract surgeons.

Quality

During the war, both Union and Confederate surgeons had to pass an exam to be appointed to their positions, helping to ensure an adequate level of care for the soldiers. In practice, many men were commissioned who had questionable abilities. Examining boards were set up at both the national and state levels. Examinations for a federal position were often more stringent, but each state had its own expectations and requirements.

The individual states were asked to organize volunteer regiments and to assign physicians for each of the regiments. While some states were conscientious in appointing the regimental surgeons and assistant surgeons, other states chose men based more on political considerations than on professional ability. Some of the early commissions were given without proof of medical training or ability. This problem was at its worst early in the war, when many people (on both sides) assumed the conflict would result in a quick and decisive victory (for their side, of course).

The quality of doctors serving in the war mirrors the quality of the soldiers. The early patriotic fervor caused many who were unfit for service to attempt to sign on for the cause. Although army regulations required that all new recruits receive a thorough physical exam at the time of their enlistment, in reality the exam was often very superficial. This circumstance allowed recruits to enter the army with chronic diseases and physical defects that would affect their performance as a soldier. While some examining surgeons were conscientious, others were less so, allowing unsuitable men (and a number of women) into the army.

When it became clear that the war was not going to be over quickly and that having unfit soldiers was a severe burden on the army, examining surgeons became more careful concerning who they allowed to enlist. In addition, most states became more serious about examining the candidates for surgeon and assistant surgeon. Lessons had been learned, but unfortunately those lessons included the loss of life. As the war progressed and the number of men willing to enlist dwindled, both the North and South resorted to instituting a draft to secure the large number of soldiers needed. Once again the standards declined--age, height and weight restrictions were loosened, and men became soldiers whether or not they were mentally and physically fit for the task.

Surgeon Duties

The vast majority of army physicians who served in the Civil War were the volunteer surgeons who served with an individual regiment. Most regiments had one regimental surgeon and one or two assistant surgeons. The regimental surgeon was responsible for coordinating the activities of the regiment with the other officers and was consulted concerning the more difficult cases of injury or disease. During the battle he was usually stationed in the field hospital, where he performed most of the amputations.

The assistant surgeon was usually younger than the surgeon and was responsible for the day-to-day medical activity of the regiment. These duties included surgeon's call, filling out forms, and requesting medical supplies. The morning surgeon's call was when members of the regiment who were ill reported for treatment. After surgeon's call, the next duty was to make the rounds of the tents and treat the men who were too sick to report to the surgeon, but not sick enough to be sent to the hospital. During a battle the assistant surgeon was given the dangerous duty of manning the field dressing station, usually on or near the battlefield. All of these volunteer surgeons gave up their private practices to serve in their regiments.

Aside from attending to the wounded after battles, the regimental surgeons were also expected to inspect the camps, supervise the hospitals, and enforce the sanitary measures required to maintain the health of the soldiers. The surgeons stressed the importance of sanitation in the army camps and cleanliness in the hospitals, but putting their ideas into practice was difficult. They often met with resistance from the line officers, and since the surgeons' ranks pertained only to the Medical

Introduction

Department, their requests were often ignored. Basically, any non-medical commissioned officer had more authority than they did.

"Sawbones"

The modern perception of Civil War surgeons is that of a "sawbones" who was relatively incompetent and who amputated arms and legs without a second thought. Civil War soldiers often held the same view of their surgeons, judging from the comments often found in diaries and letters. Fear played a large role in this perception—the truth is that while some surgeons may have overused the scalpel and saw, most were providing the best care they could given the daunting circumstances.

Just prior to the Civil War, a new type of rifled musket and bullet were developed that increased the severity of the injuries to the soldiers. The old style smooth-bore musket had a limited range and fired a round ball of lead that usually broke the skin and fractured bone. The new musket had a rifled barrel and fired a conical bullet with a hollow grooved base, called the Minié ball. They had a much longer range and better accuracy, and the projectiles traveled faster than those from smooth-bore muskets. The ball could inflict considerable damage to both bone and soft tissue due to its tendency to spin away from its long axis. Ricocheting or flattened bullets could create extensive lacerations and even carry foreign material into the wound. The extensive damage done by the Minié ball, plus its tendency to contaminate the wound, caused a dramatic increase in the development of infection.

The principal surgical procedure performed during the Civil War was amputation, accounting for three out of every four operations. When estimates from both the Confederate and Union sides are combined, about 50,000 amputations were done throughout the war, which left the surgeons open to harsh criticism and earned them the reputation of butchers. However, the poor physical condition of their patients, the large number of wounded awaiting treatment after a battle, the likelihood of developing secondary infections, and the severe nature of the wounds caused by the Minié ball made amputation the most practical procedure to follow.

Bad Doctors

Jonathan Letterman, Medical Director of the Army of the Potomac, said it best:

> "The surgery of these battle-fields has been pronounced butchery. Gross misrepresentations of the conduct of medical officers have been made and scattered broadcast over the country, causing deep and heart-rending anxiety to those who had friends or relatives in the army, who might at any moment require the services of a surgeon...If any objection could be urged against the surgery of those fields, it would be the efforts on the part of surgeons to practice 'conservative surgery' to too great an extent."

The Ways Out

There were five ways an officer could leave the service: being mustered out with his unit; resigning; court-martial; direct dismissal; and death. Three were honorable; the other two were not. Regiments served for a specified time, so being mustered out with the regiment was common. Resignation was another option (for officers only), but the resignation had to be approved by the War Department, and the reason for resigning could not be frivolous. Death was the third honorable exit.

As for the dishonorable means, they were court-martial and direct dimissal. If an officer was found guilty of a major offense in a general court-martial, he could be cashiered--the equivalent of a dishonorable discharge. The direct dismissals are the most mysterious since there is little paperwork available. It appears that the official court-martial route was skipped and the officers were dismissed by their superiors for a variety of offenses. Many later had their dismissals revoked. Civilian doctors could have their contracts annulled, and often were blacklisted by the Medical Department.

Unfortunately for the soldiers and the surgeons, the Civil War was fought just years before the widespread acceptance of the Germ Theory and the understanding of antisepsis and the sterilization of instruments and equipment. The surgeons performed their work as best they could, but did not have the knowledge of the role germs played in causing infection.

Introduction

The surgeons were asked to perform their duties under very difficult conditions, both during and after battles and on the march and in camp. While the majority of them performed admirably, the stress they were under caused some to succumb to the pressure. Couple the stress with the surgeons' access to medicinal alcohol, and the results could be disastrous. Drunkenness, incompetence, malpractice, cowardice, and even psychological problems were all cause for proceedings against army surgeons. These "bad doctors" are listed in this volume.

Sources

Adams George W., *Doctors in Blue: the Medical History of the Union Army in the Civil War*; Collier, 1985 (first printing 1952)

Bollet, Alfred Jay; *Civil War Medicine: Challenges and Triumphs*; Galen Press, Tucson, AZ, 2002

Cunningham, H. H.; *Doctors in Gray: the Confederate Medical Service*; Louisiana State University Press, Baton Rouge, 1993 (first printing 1958)

Dorwart, Bonnie Brice; *Death is in the Breeze: Disease during the American Civil War*; NMCWM Press, 2009

Flannery, Michael A.; "Another House Divided: Union Medical Service and Sectarians During the Civil War;" *Journal of the History of Medicine*: 54 (Oct. 1999)

Grace, William; *The Army Surgeon's Manual*; 1864; reprinted 1992, Norman Publishing Co., San Francisco

Hambrecht, F. Terry; introduction to the reprinting of *Roster of Regimental Surgeons and Assistant Surgeons in the U.S. Army Medical Department During the Civil War*; Olde Soldier Books, 1989

Lowry, Thomas P. and Jack D. Welsh; *Tarnished Scalpels: The Court-Martials of Fifty Union Surgeons*; Stackpole Books, 2000

Lowry, Thomas P.; *Utterly Worthless: One Thousand Delinquent Union Officers Unworthy of a Court-Martial;* Thomas P. Lowry, 2010

The Medical and Surgical History of the Civil War, prepared by Surgeon General Joseph K. Barnes, 1870; reprinted 1991, Broadfoot Publishing Co., Wilmington, N.C. (originally titled *Medical and Surgical History of the War of the Rebellion 1861-1865*)

Ordronaux, John; *Hints on the Preservation of Health in Armies* and *Manual of Instructions for Military Surgeons on the Examination of Recruits and Discharge of Soldiers*; 1863; reprinted 1990, Norman Publishing Co., San Francisco

Reimer, Terry; *Divided by Conflict United by Compassion: The National Museum of Civil War Medicine*; NMCWM Press, 2004

Slawson, Robert G., "Medical Training in the United States Prior to the Civil War," *Surgeon's Call: The Journal of the NMCWM*; in four volumes, Vol. 7, No. 4, Vol. 8, No. 1, Vol. 8, No.2, Vol. 8 No. 3, Winter, Spring, Summer, Fall 2003.

Slawson, Robert G.; *Prologue to Change: African Americans in Medicine in the Civil War Era*; The NMCWM Press, 2006

Strait, Newton Allen; *Roster of Regimental Surgeons and Assistant Surgeons in the U.S. Army Medical Department During the Civil War;* 1882; reprinted by Norman Publishing Co. as *List of Battles and Roster of Regimental Surgeons*, San Francisco, 1990

Chapter One

The Roster

Adamides, A. D.
    Contract surgeon. Removed for AWOL. BL.
Adams, Andrew.
    Asst. Surgeon. 17th Missouri. Dismissed May 1863. Applied for a pension in 1880. RRS.
Adams, J. R.
    Asst. Surgeon. 58th Indiana. Drunk while tending the wounded at Stone's River. Acquitted. (MM177).
Adams, Z. B.
    Surgeon. 12th Massachusetts. Court-martialed twice. Gave testimony in a "light and frivolous manner." Reprimanded. (KK550). Refused colonel's order to put a wounded man in an ambulance. Dismissed. (KK752). Could this be Zabdiel Boylston Adams of the 32nd Massachusetts, an often-wounded hero of the Battle of Gettysburg? (See his biography by Charles N. Peabody, published in 1984 by the Boston Medical Library.)
Ainsworth, Richard M.
    Asst. Surgeon, later Surgeon. 11th Kansas Cavalry. Dismissed July 21, 1865. Applied for a pension in 1891 while living in Oklahoma. RRS.
Akin, W.
    Asst. Surgeon. 125th New York. Gave out blank passes on the march to Fredericksburg. Reprimanded. (NN3924).

Bad Doctors

Alleben, W. G.
   Contract surgeon. Removed for "incompetence." BL.

Allen, Benjamin Thayer.
   Contract surgeon. Removed for "intemperance." BL.

Allen, Lyman.
   Surgeon. 5th US Colored Troops. He attended "a full course of medical lectures," then enlisted as a private in the 41st Ohio Infantry. After two years of soldiering he took and passed the examination for assistant surgeon of colored troops. He was tried for being slow to see a severely wounded man. He was convicted of "inhumanity" but not of "gross inhumanity," and returned to duty. The record is filled with contradictory testimony. In 1897 he received a pension for rheumatism. He died at the Yountville Veteran's Home in 1919, in California's wine country. TS. (LL3199).

Ames, Fisher.
   Surgeon. 14th US Colored Troops. Failed to attend a wounded man. Stole hospital canned fruit and sugar. Killed a patient by a cold bath. Acquitted. (NN3618).

Anderson, Samuel H.
   A Confederate surgeon tried by the Union and sentenced to death. See Special Cases.

Andreon, Stephen W.
   Asst. Surgeon. US Volunteers. At St. Louis Smallpox Hospital, allowed soldiers to plunder. Charged civilians for treatment at the Pest House. Acquitted. (OO1259).

Angle, John S.
   Asst. Surgeon. 123rd Pennsylvania. AWOL 69 days at Sharpsburg. He'd been sick but had not requested permission to leave. Dismissed. (KK634 and MM78).

Armington, J. L.
   Asst. Surgeon. Minnesota Independent Battery. Made a false muster at Pombina, Dakota Territory. Acquitted. (LL2721).

Armstrong, Henry A.
   Surgeon. 2nd New York Heavy Artillery. He was tried for failing to diagnose a case of smallpox, for keeping a single woman in his tent, and for escorting a well-known bordello madam to Grover's

The Roster

Theatre in Washington, DC. He also killed a patient with an overdose of anesthetic. He was suspended from rank and pay for two months, and drifted into contract surgeon work at six locations until his contract was annulled. Two decades after the war he was committed to an insane asylum, which engendered decades of litigation. TS. (MM753).

Arthur, Christopher.
Surgeon. 75th Indiana. AWOL at Chattanooga. He'd been captured and starved. Acquitted. (NN1367).

Avery, Amos Green.
Contract surgeon. Removed for being "totally unqualified." BL.

Avery, Lafayette.
Asst. Surgeon. 3rd Missouri Cavalry. Dismissed 12/30/64 for habitual drunkenness and neglect of duty. UW.

Baggalt, G. W. Contract surgeon, removed for disobedience of orders. BL.

Bailey, William A.
Surgeon. 186th New York. Failed to provide ambulances. Failed to attend brigade review. Handled a woman's breasts. Acquitted. (MM2203).

Balcom, Hermogene.
Contract surgeon. Removed 6/1/64 for being drunk. Later rehired as assistant surgeon for 31st Wisconsin.

Baldwin, N. A.
Asst. Surgeon. 173rd New York. Drunk on duty. Cashiered. General Court Martial Orders, Dept. of the Gulf, 1864. GO No. 49, April 19, 1864.

Baldwin, Peter Arthur.
Contract surgeon. Removed 12/7/64 for "disreputable practice." BL. See Special Cases Chapter.

Barr, Benjamin.
Contract surgeon. Removed 9/10/64 for being incompetent. Later commissioned as surgeon for the 199th Pennsylvania. BL.

Barr, Robert.
Surgeon. 67th Pennsylvania. The court-martial record is lost. He is too sick to stay in the army, but without the court-martial record, he cannot be discharged, nor can he resign. (NN150).

Bartman (?), C. H.
   Contract surgeon. Removed 12/31/63 by order of the Medical Dept. BL.
Bates, D. T.
   Contract surgeon. Removed 4/4/65 for drunkenness and neglect of duty. BL.
Bates, Henry G.
   Asst. Surgeon. 131st New York. Drunk on parade at Annapolis. Drunk on the steamer *United States*. Stole twenty bottles of whiskey, sold them to sailors. Cashiered. (MM661). Went on a three-week drunk on New Orleans, refused to treat colored troops. Dismissed (again?). (LL1073 and NN857).
Bauman, Isaac.
   Contract surgeon. Removed 10/31/63 by order of Surgeon-General William A. Hammond. BL.
Baxter, Andrew James.
   Asst. Surgeon. US Army Medical staff. Dismissed January 19, 1863 "…after serving for seventeen months." Enlisted in Ohio. *Heitman*.
Beans, Richard Albert.
   Contract surgeon. Removed 11/1/64 for "inefficiency." He was later rehired on 1/17/65. BL.
Beatty, J. E.
   Surgeon. 2nd Maryland Veteran Volunteers. AWOL seven days at Christmas. Fined seven days pay. (MM3589).
Bell, William S.
   Asst. Surgeon. 43rd Ohio. Only data: his dismissal was revoked and commission restored 1/4/64. UW.
Benedict, Michael D.
   Surgeon. 75th New York. Only data: dismissal revoked. UW.
Bennet, Sevilla A.
   Asst. Surgeon. 20th Maine. Messed with enlisted men. Ate enlisted men's food. Did not pay his maintenance. Ate with a musician but did not pay his share. Dismissed. (LL257).
Benson, Julius A.
   Asst. Surgeon. 7th Indiana Cavalry. Drunk much of five months at Memphis. Drank hospital whiskey. At the Battle of White's Station,

The Roster

took all the medical supplies and ran to Memphis. Cashiered. (NN3317).

Berkley, B. F.
Contract surgeon. Removed 5/25/64 for neglect of duty. BL.

Beshler, J. B.
Asst. Surgeon. 81st Pennsylvania. Failed to treat patients for four days at Bolivar Heights. Acquitted. (LL57).

Bettleheim (Bettelheim), Bernard J.
Surgeon. 106th Illinois. His regiment seethed with ill will. A major factor was Dr. Bettleheim, accused of: (1) proclaiming a man well, only 72 hours before the man's death; (2) sending his orderlies to fish for him; and (3) loudly complaining that the regiment's commanders were drunkards. Bettleheim told the court that he could not "understand the customs of America." He was sentenced to be dismissed from the service. At the same time, a medical examining board found him "unqualified." TS. (LL1411).

Bidluck, W. W.
Asst. Surgeon. 62nd New York. Refused to take an examination. Dismissed. (LL280 and LL234).

Bing, J. P.
Asst. Surgeon. 53rd Ohio. Deserted two months at Shiloh, Tennessee. Acquitted. (KK333).

Bischoff, John.
Contract surgeon. Removed 5/19/64 for incompetence and neglect of duty. BL.

Biser, Tilgman.
Contract surgeon. Removed 10/20/64 for drunkenness. BL.

Blaisdell, W.
Contract surgeon. Removed 10/24/64 for "cowardice." BL.

Blaisdell, Wesley.
See Special Cases chapter. (Same man as W. Blaisdell?)

Blanchard, Enoch.
Surgeon. 7th Vermont. At Pensacola he was accused of eating hospital food paid for by the "hospital fund." The cook testified that Blanchard had paid for the food, and had, in fact, purchased more food for the hospital. "Before Dr. Blanchard came, we lived on salt junk. Now we have potatoes, onions, butter and

milk." After much petty quibbling, he was acquitted. Post-war, he suffered from malaria, probably from his time in the South. TS. (KK661).

Boemer, Edmund.
Surgeon. 4th Missouri. This was a mostly German regiment. He was charged with profiting from the regimental food. An accounting nightmare was not helped by Army regulations in English, given to men who knew only German. The cook told the court that Boemer had asked him to make out a bill for the food consumed by the doctor, but the cook could not read or write in either language. After much testimony over eggs, Boemer was convicted and dismissed. The court documents tell us that some patients were issued "water soup." TS. (LL457).

Bolton, J. Henry.
Asst. Surgeon. 7th Maryland. AWOL seven days from a leave of absence at Culpeper, Virginia. "I went home to get married." Fined one months' pay. (NN3927).

Boone, Jermingham.
Surgeon. 1st Maryland Potomac Home Brigade. He made thirteen fraudulent ration returns and was dishonorably dismissed. (OO893).

Boughton, Henry J.
Contract surgeon. Removed 4/4/65 for drunkenness and "conduct prejudicial to good order and military discipline." BL.

Bowen, Julius C.
Contract surgeon. Removed 9/1/64 for "unsatisfactory performance of duty." BL.

Bowers, William P.
Asst. Surgeon. 2nd Arkansas. Dismissed September 22, 1864. Age 33 at enlistment. RRS.

Bowman, Charles.
Contract surgeon. Removed 6/1/64 for "refusal to obey orders." BL.

Brackett, J. W.
Contract surgeon. Removed 7/2/64 for conveying letters to Confederate prisoners of war. BL.

The Roster

Bradish, James S.
> Asst. Surgeon. 146th New York. Dismissed May 6, 1863. Commissioned February 1863 at age 36. Pre-war residence was Lowville, NY. Died at Hilton Head, SC. RRS.

Bradley, Jacob W.
> Contract surgeon. Removed 1/11/64 for "habitual carelessness." Taken off Black List 5/26/76. BL.

Bradley, William Alfred.
> Asst. Surgeon. Regular Army. Drunk on the march to Fairfax Courthouse. Acquitted. Brevetted major in 1865 for "faithful and meritorious service." Died 1869. (II782).

Brewer, D. R.
> At Baltimore, this civilian doctor counterfeited Confederate currency and bonds, and smuggled cotton cards to the South. He received two years at hard labor. (NN3717).

Briggs, Charles E.
> Surgeon. 54th Massachusetts Infantry (colored). A young private was accused of sexual intercourse with a horse. Briggs' testimony help acquit the soldier. However… the next night, Briggs kidnapped the soldier, had him tied down, and circumcised him without anesthetic. Briggs' court-martial never took place, perhaps because of his Harvard network of political friends. He died in 1894, at Boston. TS.

Brooks, Theodore D.
> Asst. Surgeon. 38th Ohio. Dismissed 4/18/65 (at age 24) for disobedience, AWOL, and failure to appear before commission. Dismissal later revoked. UW.

Brother, Ferdinand.
> Surgeon. 8th Cavalry, Missouri State Militia. Regimental musters included horses as well as men. Brother was charged with keeping a false muster – he listed a horse as present, when the horse was, in fact, dead. The basis of the charge was perjury by the adjutant, who bore a grudge. Brother was acquitted, survived the war, and died at his Nebraska home in 1920. TS. (LL1980).

Bad Doctors

Brown, John T.
> Asst. Surgeon. US Volunteers. Paid a bribe to be transferred to Baltimore. Acquitted. Prior service in the 105th New York and the 94th New York. Brevetted major in 1865 for "faithful and effective service." (NN3081).

Brown, P. B.
> Contract surgeon. Removed 7/19/64 for drunkenness. BL.

Brown, W. T.
> Contract surgeon. Removed 12/20/64 for incompetence and disobedience of orders. BL.

Brown, William A.
> Contract surgeon. Removed 2/25/65 for neglect of duty. BL.

Browne, Henry W.
> Surgeon. 76th US Colored Troops. He was AWOL two months, due to severe diarrhea and debility. Acquitted. (OO1432).

Brundage, A. H.
> Asst. Surgeon. 32nd Ohio. Sold government whiskey to soldiers. Sold a barrel of government flour for $10 ($300 to $1000 today) and kept the money. Said, "Old Abe and this Congress couldn't send the nation to hell." Boasted he could get rid of officers. Dismissed. (LL3232).

Buchanan, James B.
> Surgeon. 32nd Ohio. His first contact with the 32nd Ohio was a telegram saying he was too drunk to travel. After he arrived, a dozen witnesses said he was constantly drunk. One recollected him sleeping through a battle. Other witnesses described sobriety or moderation. Further witnesses said he stole the good food to feed his wife and children. He was dismissed by Abraham Lincoln, but re-instated into the 125th Ohio by the governor and served into 1865. TS. (II1000).

Buck, Ephraim W.
> Asst. Surgeon. 81st New York. Dismissed 1/4/64 after failing to appear before commission. Restored three months later. Also served in 9th and 51st New York. Brevetted major in 1865. UW.

Buel, W. P.
> Surgeon. 131st New York. Passed out drunk, lost his medical instruments. Beat up a sick soldier at Difficult Creek, Virginia. Stole Sanitary Commission food. Dismissed. (LL2940).

The Roster

Bull, John Smith.
: Contract surgeon. Removed 2/15/65 for cowardice and insubordination. BL.

Bunkley, J. Thomas.
: Contract surgeon. Removed 4/11/65 for "worthlessness." BL.

Burg, Washington.
: Asst. Surgeon. 122nd Pennsylvania. Only data: dismissal revoked 5/16/63. Honorably discharged. Also served in 207th Pennsylvania. UW.

Burgess, C. H.
: Contract surgeon. (Not in *Heitman* or civilwardata.com). Gave a soldier a fake ID, allowed him to collect $248 of another man's money. Reprimanded. Gen. Augur furious at light sentence. (LL2866).

Burke, George.
: Asst. Surgeon. 46th Pennsylvania. He was told to send the wounded by train, but sent them on foot. Reprimanded. (LL1062).

Burke, W. R.
: Surgeon. US Volunteers. He charged twenty-five cents to fill out a certificate of disability, at Cairo, Illinois. Acquitted. (KK176).

Burnett, J. W.
: Contract surgeon. Removed 7/27/64 for "disloyalty." BL.

Burnham, Alfred M.
: Asst. Surgeon. 10th Minnesota. Dismissed October 23, 1863. Commissioned in October 1862 at age 38. Post-war residence: Albert Lea, MN. RRS.

Burt, George.
: Surgeon. US Volunteers. Only data: Dismissal revoked. Died 1882. UW.

Bussey, Harvey.
: Contract surgeon. Removed 10/22/63 for AWOL. BL.

Buswell, Albert.
: Contract surgeon. Removed 2/23/63 with note: "Not to be recontacted with," but was rehired 4/22/65. BL.

Cady, Charles E.
: Surgeon. 128th Pennsylvania. Dismissal revoked after meeting a board of officers. Prior service in 121st Pennsylvania. UW.

Cake, William M.
   Surgeon. 53rd Ohio. He placed his hospital outside Union lines. Acquitted. (NN3831).
Campbell, Charles Fitz.
   Surgeon. US Volunteers. Dishonorably mustered out 6/3/65. Reason not recorded. Prior service in 23rd Pennsylvania. UW.
Campbell, William K.
   Contract surgeon. Removed 4/9/65 for drunkenness. BL.
Carlisle, Eber S.
   Asst. Surgeon. 186th New York. Drunk. Neglected a wounded soldier. Signed false ration returns. Never studied or received a degree. Gave whiskey to enlisted men. Acquitted. (NN3063).
Carlisle, Zachariah.
   Contract surgeon. Removed 10/31/63 with note: "Not to be employed again." BL.
Carpenter, Horace.
   Surgeon. 1st Oregon. At Fort Stevens, Oregon, beat a sergeant and a captain with his cane. Went to Astoria without permission. Acquitted. (MM3200).
Carr, Josiah.
   Surgeon. 30th Maine Veteran Volunteers. Dismissal revoked July 1864. Prior service in 25th Maine. UW.
Carstens, John F.
   Contract surgeon. Removed 10/23/64 for "incompetence." BL.
Carter, John C.
   Asst. Surgeon. 4th Maryland. Dismissal revoked after defending his case. Later served in US Volunteers. UW.
Case, Calvin D.
   Asst. Surgeon. 180th Ohio. Dismissed 4/22/65 for AWOL and failing to meet with commission. UW.
Castleman, Alfred L.
   Surgeon. 5th Wisconsin. He obtained his commission on the basis of: (1) an honorary MD from the University of Wisconsin; (2) a medical license issued by the town of Vincennes, Indiana; (3) a letter from a clergyman that he had seen a diploma with Castleman's name on it; and (4) a demand from the governor of Wisconsin that Castleman be commissioned. Five months after

The Roster

joining the regiment he was charged with feeding his horse government hay, charging patients for their medicines, and restricting the prescribing of another doctor. It appears that he had paid for hay, that he had purchased the medicine with his own funds, and that the restricted doctor has prescribed dangerous levels of mercury. He was acquitted of every charge. At Antietam, he acquired a flesh-eating infection and, in December 1862, resigned. His destitute widow died in California in 1893. TS. (KK499).

Caswell, Walter C.
Asst. Surgeon. 101st Ohio. Failed to treat seriously wounded men. Acquitted, "…but it is clear that some of the wounded were grossly neglected." Seventy pages of testimony. (LL584).

Clark, Augustus M.
Surgeon. US Volunteers. He was in charge of a hospital at Falmouth, Virginia. He was accused of returning a very sick man to duty, where he died six days later. Prosecution witnesses said the sick man had such severe diarrhea that he fouled the hospital, and that Clark had sent him away because his excreta made a nuisance. A Dr. Ramsey testified that the dead man was having only "six evacuations" a day, but about to receive a medical discharge from the army. Clark was acquitted. The dying man spent his last days lying out on the ground, in the sun and rain, without a tent or a blanket. TS. (LL326).

Clark, Elijah A.
Surgeon. US Volunteers. Dismissed 4/28/65. Reason not recorded. Prior service in the 37th Illinois and was promoted to surgeon in the 8th Missouri Cavalry. UW.

Clark, Luke W.
This civilian doctor visited the camp of the 151st Illinois, where his brother was very sick with syphilis. He felt his brother was treated incorrectly and prescribed for him, which infuriated the regimental surgeon. Dr. Clark was fined $100, roughly $5,000 today. (MM3396).

Classon, C. P.
Contract surgeon. Removed 12/22/63 "by order of the Surgeon-General." BL.

Clemmons, Leonidis D.
>Surgeon. 61st Illinois. Drunkenness at Pittsburgh Landing and Bolivar, Tennessee. Asked, "Is there fucking to be had here among the Negro women?" Cashiered. (NN3930).

Cobb, John W.
>Surgeon. 134th Pennsylvania. He was ordered to escort a number of wounded men from Stoneman's Switch, Stafford County, Virginia, to Aquia Creek, and see that they safely boarded a steamboat bound for Washington, DC. He was then to promptly return. Instead, he went to Pennsylvania for five weeks, and was court-martialed for AWOL. After hearing his somewhat flimsy excuses, the court acquitted him. The reviewer, Brig. Gen. A. A. Humphreys, a stickler for detail, waxed apoplectic and returned the case to the court, which refused to change their verdict. Humphrey's scathing denunciation was to no avail. Several months later, Cobb claimed a possibly spurious injury, and on the basis of a very doubtful disability report, Cobb or his descendants received money from the taxpayers until 1929. He had served seven months. TS. (LL231).

Cobb, Stephen M.
>Asst. Surgeon. 35th Iowa. AWOL one month. He had intermittent fever, bloating, diarrhea, and facial neuralgia. Acquitted. (MM1265).

Cole, W. C. (William?).
>Contract surgeon. Removed 12/17/64 for "physical disability." BL.

Collins, E. B.
>Surgeon. 51st Indiana. At Chattanooga, wrote an insulting letter to a captain, calling him a drunk and a sneak. Acquitted. (OO1125).

Collins, O. C.
>This civilian doctor was charged with stealing lumber from the Union Smallpox Hospital at Macon, Georgia. He was acquitted. (MM3396).

Collis, Robert W.
>Contract surgeon. Removed 3/20/65 for "bad habits." BL.

The Roster

Colton, Charles.
> Asst. Surgeon. 17th US Infantry. Failed to attend Pvt. Melvin Wade, who died in his tent at Falmouth, Virginia, of diarrhea. "The captain failed to provide a tent. [Wade] was too filthy to share a tent … filthy with vermin and had urine and excrement on him." Acquitted. (NN53).

Comer, S. L.
> Contract surgeon. Removed 7/16/?? for disobedience. BL.

Conover, R. A.
> Surgeon. 108th Illinois. Charged with AWOL. Evidence showed him too sick with diarrhea to travel. Acquitted. (LL2051).

Cook, Archibald B.
> Contract surgeon. Removed 8/5/63 for disloyalty and inefficiency. BL.

Cook, James.
> Surgeon. He was postmaster at Chaptico, Maryland. Smuggled letters South. Court decision not known. (NN1897).

Cook, William.
> Surgeon. 23rd New Jersey. In Maryland, drunk on hospital whiskey, refused to let ambulances carry the sick. Reprimanded. (NN3930).

Cooper, H. S.
> Contract surgeon. Removed 10/3/64 for incompetence. BL.

Cooper, Willam H. (or M.)
> Asst. Surgeon. 6th New Jersey. Dismissed November 20, 1862. RRS.

Coover, Joseph H.
> Contract surgeon. Removed 5/17/64. "Not to be employed again." BL.

Cornish, Aaron.
> Asst. Surgeon. 97th New York. Dismissed September 8, 1862. Enlisted at age 28 in October 1861. RRS.

Cowles, Edward O.
> Asst. Surgeon. 15th Connecticut. Stayed out overnight. The surgeon gave him permission. Court lenient, "as no intent to disobey." Reprimanded (LL1142).

Crandall, Owen H.
    Asst. Surgeon. 21st Missouri Veteran Volunteers. AWOL. Acquitted. He had dysentery. Also served in 24th Missouri. (LL3316).
Crandall, W. B.
    Surgeon. 33rd US Colored Troops. Submitted a false travel voucher for the sick at Charleston, South Carolina. Suspended from rank and pay for a month. Review general spares him, citing honorable service to the city's poor as well as his soldier patients. (MM3281).
Crawford, William H.
    Asst. Surgeon. 1st US Colored Troops. Dismissed August 1864. Post-war residence: Nazareth, PA. RRS.
Croghan, Patrick.
    Contract surgeon. Removal date not recorded. "Drunk." BL.
Crosby, Thomas H.
    Surgeon. 47th Indiana. AWOL twenty days. Acquitted. (LL2038).
Crouse, William B.
    See Special Cases chapter. 37th & 38th US Colored Troops. BL. UW.
Crowell, Reuben.
    Contract surgeon. Removed 6/30/65. Reason not recorded. BL.
Culver, William W.
    Asst. Surgeon. 56th Pennsylvania. AWOL six days at Fredericksburg. Acquitted. (LL58).
Cummings, J. M.
    Surgeon. 114th Pennsylvania. Drunk on duty, refused to report to headquarters. Court asks clemency. Meade approves cashiering. (MM620).
Cunan, W. H.
    Contract surgeon. Removed 6/1/64 for refusal to obey orders. BL.
Cunningham, Thurlow.
    Surgeon. 101st New York. Dismissed October 13, 1862. Commissioned October 12, 1861 at age 28. RRS.
Cutter, James.
    Contract surgeon. Removed 1/6/64 for neglect of duty. BL.
Dalton, G. F.
    Contract surgeon. 22nd Army Corps. He was AWOL a day at Washington, DC, and wrote letters outside of proper channels. He was reprimanded. (OO511).

The Roster

Davis, A. C.
 Contract surgeon. At Natchez, Mississippi he refused to report to the hospital for colored troops, and charged men to make out their discharge papers. He was reprimanded. Gen. Gilchrist ordered his contract annulled. (MM3267).

Davis, Charles.
 Asst. Surgeon. 97th Illinois. Ate some enlisted rations. Much regimental quarreling and jealousy. Acquitted. (LL394).

Davis, Jonathan E.
 Asst. Surgeon. 27th Michigan. Dismissed 1/18/64. UW.

Day, Josiah F.
 Asst. Surgeon. 19th Maine. At Darlington, South Carolina, fought with a civilian over a kettle, entered the wife's room without knocking and spoke bad language to her. "Guilty but no criminality so acquitted." (MM3427).

De Grasse, John V.
 Asst. Surgeon. 35th US Colored Troops. Drunk in Virginia. Drunk while retreating at Cedar Creek, Florida. Drunk on the steamer *Mary Benton*, where he talked dirty to a "colored woman" and assaulted her. Stole whiskey at Jacksonville, Florida. (Worth an article.) Cashiered. He was later famous as a pioneering black physician, trained in Maine and Paris. (NN2809).

De Marmon, Pierre (Paulo).
 Surgeon. "New York Sharpshooters." Had service in the 17th, 163rd, and 178th New York. Sold disability discharges for $100. Dismissed. Gen. Dix says evidence is faulty. (NN415).

De Puy, Elias C.
 Surgeon. 46th Illinois. Falsified enlistment exam for Martin Van Buren, colored, age eighteen, illiterate, who had one leg shorter than the other, at Vicksburg. Received $25 bribe. Acquitted. (LL2678).

De Wint, Frederick.
 Surgeon. 8th US Colored Troops Heavy Artillery. Dismissed October 1865. RRS.

Deale, James.
 Contract surgeon. Removed 12/13/64 for drunkenness and inefficiency. BL.

Devendorf (Davendorf), Daniel B.
> Surgeon. 19th Wisconsin. Dismissal revoked 2/18/65 after meeting with commission. UW.

Dewey, Annin W.
> Asst. Surgeon and Surgeon. 101st Indiana. Dismissed December 30, 1863. Pre-war residence: Noblesville, IN. RRS.

Dickson, John.
> Surgeon. 111th US Colored Troops. In Alabama, made an agreement with Nathan Bedford Forrest, to protect the hospital. Early 1865. Complex, fascinating story. (Worth an article.) (OO851).

Dilts, George S.
> Surgeon. 5th New York Heavy Artillery. Court of inquiry into whether he: took bribes to issue discharges, made a false muster, passed a ruptured man into the service, drank hospital whiskey, and was drunk on the streets of Baltimore. Court recommended a court-martial. Yet he was still with the regiment two years later. (NN1079).

Dixon, Lucius J.
> Surgeon. 1st Wisconsin. Tried to have the army pay for moving his food. Story is a great insight into bureaucracy. Acquitted. (KK624).

Donnell, Jotham.
> Surgeon. 15th Maine. He "… did handle the penis of Private William Seward … sick of gonorrhea, verulenta and chancre, and did immediately … examine with his fingers the throat of … another private." Donnell was also charged with not providing tents for the sick. The prosecution's witness was a "doctor" who had no diploma and had called Donnell "an old fart." Much probable perjury. He was acquitted. However, his colonel called Donnell "unfit." Donnell continued to serve with the 15th Maine until January 1865. TS. (LL297).

Donnelly, Edward.
> Surgeon, 5th Pennsylvania Reserves. He faced a court of inquiry which included George G. Meade. The charge? "Inhuman vandalism." A chaplain had reported Donnelly for picking up bones on the Manassas battlefield. Testimony showed the bones to be old and bleached, not recent. Donnelly had a long career in

The Roster

biological collecting, including West Africa and Brazil. He was acquitted. Honorable service throughout the war. Died in 1891 in one author's (TPL) hometown, Piedmont, California, but long before that author's birth. TS. (II857 and II914).

Donnler, Z. P.
Asst. Surgeon. 7th US Colored Troops. At Indianola, Texas stayed on the transport Beaufort when ordered to the quarantine station. Drunk. Acquitted. (MM3244).

Dougherty, George.
Asst. Surgeon. 59th New York. Drunk for two days at Morrisville, Virginia. Dismissed. (NN149 and NN141).

Draine, William.
Contract surgeon. Removed 4/29/64 for "general unfitness." BL.

Drake, Nelson S.
Asst. Surgeon. 16th New York Cavalry. (A scandal-ridden unit. See the author's *Tarnished Eagles*.) Drake was charged with "forming a mess with enlisted men." Drake sometimes shared a meal with his hospital steward. The court heard endless quibbling over when this constituted "a mess." He was dismissed, but re-instated by Judge Holt, Lincoln's legal adviser. Later transferred to US Volunteers. In 1865 brevetted captain for "faithful and meritorious service." Died 1880. TS. (MM1263 and LL194).

Dubois, John Coert.
Contract surgeon. Removed 9/17/64 for drunkenness. BL.

Dumreicher, C. C.
Surgeon. US Volunteers. Refused to send a hospital steward on a march at Camp Gibbs, Oregon (a grazing camp used briefly during the Snake Indian War). Sent an insubordinate letter. Acquitted. (NN3196).

Dunn, I. L.
Surgeon. "Sigel's Division." Just before a battle he received an order that took all the ambulance horses. "The colonel is a goddam fool and an idiot. He has no goddam right to do this." Dunn was dismissed. (KK66).

Ebersole, Jacob.
    Surgeon. 19th Indiana. AWOL two days at Belle Plain, Virginia. The train was late. Acquitted. (LL133).

Edmanson, John A.
    Contract surgeon. Removed 1/30/65 for "inattention to duty and insubordination." BL.

Eisenlord, Alonza M.
    Surgeon. 7th New York. From the record, he appears to have been a very unpleasant person. In his service with the 7th New York Infantry, he stole money, hoarded food, and stole home food parcels. He also hid needed medical supplies in his tent, saying there were none. He kept food in his tent until it rotted. A dozen witnesses confirmed his misdeeds. A first-rate chronophage, he even got Lincoln involved. He was acquitted. TS. (II773 and II447).

Elliott, W. W.
    Surgeon. 11th Michigan. Made out duplicate discharge papers for a private at Murfreesboro. Reprimanded. (LL278).

Ellis, G. W.
    Contract surgeon. Removed 10/31/64 for drunkenness. BL.

Ellsberry, Isaac N.
    Asst. Surgeon. 16th Ohio. Submitted his resignation outside of proper channels, his prior attempt being ignored. He was very sick. Reprimanded. (MM295).

Ensey, John B.
    Surgeon. 5th Illinois Cavalry. Drunk on duty at three locations in Mississippi. Acquitted. (OO111).

Evans, Owen J.
    Asst. Surgeon. At White Sulfur Springs, Virginia, made a false certificate of disability. Acquitted. (NN3869).

Farish, James.
    Contract surgeon. Dismissed 11/2/64 for "inefficiency." Later, commissioned assistant surgeon in the 13th Maryland Infantry. BL.

The Roster

Fawcett, Richard W.
Asst. Surgeon. 155th New York. Failed surgeon's call at Fairfax Courthouse, Virginia. He was sick. Acquitted. (NN409). He died of disease seven months later.

Fay, Hallett.
Contract surgeon. Removed 6/9/64 for "incompetence." BL.

Feam, Herbert.
Asst. Surgeon. 44th New York. At Aldie, Virginia, refused to return a horse. Acquitted. (NN3942).

Feehan, Edward L.
Surgeon. 10th Missouri Cavalry. The colonel of the regiment returned at 3:00 AM on a cold rainy night to find the doctor had eaten much of the food and was sleeping dry and comfortable in the colonel's place. Further, the doctor had failed to report a plot to kill the colonel. The doctor had left all his wounded in ambulances at the bottom of the mud-soaked hill, while he slept warm and dry on top of the hill. The court acquitted him of neglect, but the reviewing general ordered Feehan reprimanded. Feehan deserted and went to Ireland. Dismissed 3/12/64. TS. UW. (LL683).

Ferguson, John C.
Asst. Surgeon. 7th Ohio. Dismissed 10/19/63 after eight months service. Probably re-instated since he was mustered out in July 1864. UW.

Fields, John W.
Civilian employee of George W. Smith's Maryland Cavalry. Fields issued a false surgeon's certificate. The trial is a tangle of legal obfuscation. Decision: the court has no jurisdiction. (LL433).

Finley, Clement A.
Surgeon-General of the US Army. He had been court-martialed twice before the war, over petty territorial issues, in trials that involved Braxton Bragg, William Beaumont, Winfield Scott, and Millard Fillmore. Finley represented the old army – short-sighted, narrow, parochial, bitter, and penurious. In a bit of political guerrilla warfare involving George B. McClellan, Simon Cameron, the Sanitary Commission, and Charles S. Tripler, Finley lost out. The

real winner was the average wounded soldier, who would now receive better care. TS. (II547).

Fischer, Charles A.
Contract surgeon. Removed 11/26/64 for disobedience. BL.

Fisher, James.
Surgeon. US Volunteers. Dismissed. Dismissal revoked in January 1864. Honorably mustered out January 1865. Died 1880. UW.

Fisher, Orange.
Contract surgeon. Removed 1/16/64 "by order of Surgeon G. Perrin." BL.

Fleming, William J.
Surgeon. 102nd Pennsylvania. His case illustrates the deep flaw in Civil War medical care – reliance on the old pre-war regimental surgeon structure. If a wounded man from another regiment stumbled into the 102nd Pennsylvania he was resented, because food and medical care was allocated by regiment, not by need. In the seven days before Richmond, Fleming was not only away from his designated post but was very sick with malaria. In a system designed for dozens of wounded, there was chaos when the wounded were in the thousands, reflecting, perhaps, McClellan's capacity for grand ideas and ineptitude for carrying them out. Fleming was convicted of being absent from his post and dismissed. TS. (KK91).

Fleming, William.
Contract surgeon. Removed 6/25/65 for drunkenness. BL.

Flore, Frederick.
Asst. Surgeon. 1st Missouri State Guards, a Confederate unit. Convicted of lurking. Sentenced to hard labor to the end of the war. (NN1910).

Floyd, Theodore S.
Contract surgeon. Removed 12/10/63 for "incompetence." BL.

Flynn, Edward.
Contract surgeon. At St. Louis, Missouri, was accused of accepting money to make false diagnoses of heart disease in men seeking a discharge. The testimony revealed a wide variety of conflicting medical opinions and confusing terms (what was "torpidity of the liver"?), plus the strong possibility

The Roster

that Flynn had been the victim of a sting operation. He was convicted, dismissed, and sentenced to sixty days in prison. Several reviewers came to his defense, with very limited success. Eighteen years later he was refused a pension. TS. (LL930 and LL932).

Fogg, Benjamin.
   Contract surgeon. Removed 11/25/63 "by order of the Secretary of War [Edwin M. Stanton]." BL.

Foster, Christian.
   Surgeon. 58th Ohio. At Big Black River, Mississippi, neglected the sick for three weeks, gave US medicine to Vicksburg civilians. Acquitted. (LL3114).

Foster, William.
   Asst. Surgeon. 13th Indiana. Dismissed October 13, 1862. Pre-war residence: Bloomington, IN. RRS.

Foster, F. J.
   Asst. Surgeon. 13th Illinois Cavalry. AWOL two weeks at Pine Bluff, Arkansas. He had "chronic diarrhea." Acquitted. (LL2860 and NN3130).

Fox, E. C.
   Contract surgeon. Removed 5/15/64 for "ungentlemanly and disruptive conduct." BL.

Franklin, Morris J.
   Asst. Surgeon. 4th New York Cavalry. At Hunter's Chapel, Virginia, failed to give vaccinations, failed to report, claimed that men were "rotting without care or attention." Cashiered. (140 in "numbered files.")

Freeman, J. W.
   106th New York. (The *Army Register* lists two surgeons: Surgeon John N. Freeman and Asst. Surgeon Julius A. Freeman in the 106th New York.) He lied about a private servant. Long discussion of servants for officers. Acquitted. (OO426).

Freeman, William.
   Surgeon. 7th Indiana Cavalry. Dismissed May 10, 1864. Also served as Asst. Surgeon in 52nd Indiana. Post-war residence: Camden (or Pennville) IN. RRS.

Fulks, James S.
>   Contract surgeon. Removed from the army at an unrecorded date for "unsatisfactory service." BL.

Fuller, Winfield S.
>   Asst. Surgeon. 8th New York Cavalry. AWOL two days at Relay House, Maryland. "I had cholera morbus from eating fruit." Reprimanded and lost three months pay. (KK297).

Fulton, James.
>   Asst. Surgeon. 143rd Pennsylvania. Dismissed 4/19/64. Prior service in 150th Pennsylvania. Died 1919. UW.

Funkhouser, David.
>   Contract surgeon. Removed 11/9/63 for "incompetence." BL.

Galbraith, Benjamin A.
>   Contract surgeon. Removed 7/23/63. "Drunk." BL.

Gardiner, William A.
>   Surgeon. 81st Pennsylvania. His 1842 medical degree from Pennsylvania College made him more qualified than many Civil War surgeons. Charles Tripler was McClellan's medical director. Gardiner showed up drunk in Tripler's office, so drunk he could not recall events of only sixty seconds prior. He was acquitted of being drunk. (Part of the record is in shorthand.) The reviewing general disagreed, but opined that one court-martial would be a sobering experience. Wrong. Gardiner continued to drink until placed in an insane asylum, where he died in 1863 of delirium tremens. His widow received a pension until 1912. TS. (II618).

Gauntt, F.
>   Contract surgeon. Removed 3/9/65 for "conduct prejudicial to good order and military discipline." BL.

Gay, Stephen R.
>   Contract surgeon. Removed 12/24/64 for "incompetence." BL.

Gibson, H. M.
>   Contract surgeon. Removed 11/16/64 for disobedience. BL.

Gihon, John H.
>   Asst. Surgeon. 74th US Colored Troops. At Ship Island, called a lieutenant "a goddam liar and a goddam scoundrel." Acquitted. (MM2025).

The Roster

Gilbert, Alson J.
> Asst. Surgeon. 7th Illinois Cavalry. Dismissed for AWOL. Failed to appear before commission. UW.

Gilbert, P. I. (or J.)
> Asst. Surgeon. 2nd Louisiana Cavalry. Drunk on duty. Refused to examine sick men, said they were well. One died. Cursed the captain. Broke arrest. Dismissed. (NN1887).

Gilbert, Robert H.
> Contract surgeon. Removed 7/2/64 for "constant drunkenness." BL.

Gilman, Uriah.
> Asst. Surgeon. 12th New Jersey. Dismissal revoked after defending his case. Mustered out 6/4/65. UW.

Glenny, William.
> Surgeon. 49th US Colored Troops. AWOL twenty days at Vicksburg. Medical records show severe diarrhea. Acquitted. (NN3559).

Goldsborough, Charles E.
> Asst. Surgeon. 5th Maryland. Dismissed 10/17/64 for AWOL and failing to appear before commission. Dismissal revoked upon honorable discharge. Wounded at Petersburg August 1864. UW.

Goodson, John W.
> Asst. Surgeon. 72nd Ohio. Dismissed March 1863. Pre-war residence: Belleview, OH. RRS.

Gordon, Perkins.
> Surgeon. 35th Ohio. He was charged with eating in the company of enlisted men. During a long campaign through four states, Gordon shared meals, sitting outdoors, with his nurses and hospital steward. Further he was charged with mingling his cooking gear with that of the regiment, in testimony whose quibbling resembled the rules for an Orthodox kosher kitchen. Gordon had also treated his own scurvy with regimental vegetables. He was found guilty and lost a month's pay. His effort to transfer out of the 35th Ohio was ended by sunstroke. TS (LL382).

Gordon, Stewart.
> Contract surgeon. Removed 5/7/64 for "intoxication." BL.

Gorminger, William H.
> Surgeon. 27th Pennsylvania. He was charged with treating patients cruelly, during a four-week drunk. And with failing to bring medical supplies to an impending battle. And with going to Philadelphia, when he was supposed to be treating patients at Winchester, Virginia. He was acquitted. Then he deserted. Then he faked illness. Then he reappeared as surgeon of the 16th Pennsylvania Cavalry. He did not apply for a pension. TS. (KK207).

Gray, Charles.
> Surgeon. 11th New York (the Fire Zouaves). Gray's impatience with petty bureaucracy may have originated during his decorated service in the Crimean War, the Sepoy Rebellion, and some wars in China. Gray's sick and wounded were sleeping in the mud, as their tents had no floors. He wished to obtain a pass to go to Baltimore to buy floorboards, but could not go until his pass was signed by the general, John W. Phelps, a man noted for touchiness and violent opinions. Gray visited the general's headquarters, but Phelps was "not in." Gray went to Baltimore without a pass. He was convicted of AWOL, in spite of his purpose and his excellent record in combat surgery. He was sentenced to a loss of pay for a month. Soon, he was in trouble again. A patient needed whiskey for a midnight ailment. Doctors could draw no whiskey from stores without the general's signature (this time Gen. Mansfield). Gray went to the general's quarters and was arrested, most likely for annoying the general at night. In both the floorboard and whiskey issues, Gray paid the costs out of his own pocket. He seems to have been a skillful and compassionate surgeon, restrained by bureaucratic old Army types. TS. (II556).

Gray, Elias W.
> Asst. Surgeon. 58th US Colored Troops. Took bribes at Natchez for discharges. A hospital matron testified. Acquitted. (OO1495).

Gray, John W.
> Surgeon. 65th New York. He "took the pledge" not to drink. His pledge is in the file. Then he took "a little whiskey and quinine" for his malaria and got so drunk he was personally arrested by Brig. Gen. Ranald S. MacKenzie. Reprimanded and fined a months' pay. (MM1751).

The Roster

Green, Isaiah.
   At Nashville, this civilian doctor was charged with stealing and selling a government horse. He was acquitted. (MM2126).

Greene, Francis C.
   Asst. Surgeon. 30th Massachusetts. Tried to force his way past the guard to enter a private home. He defied orders not to straggle. He was impaired by morphine. (NN514).

Greene, Jerome B.
   Asst. Surgeon. 5th Rhode Island Heavy Artillery. Dismissed for AWOL and cleared by commission. UW.

Greenleaf, William A.
   Acting Asst. Surgeon. US Volunteers. He was the subject of a court of inquiry, held at Hilton Head, SC. He was accused of stealing the money of soldiers who died in his hospital. The court found that there was no system of safeguarding such money and that Greenleaf was not guilty of anything. In the South he contracted malaria and erysipelas and was sick the next thirty years. TS. (LL2258).

Greiss, Rudolph.
   Asst. Surgeon. 15th New York Heavy Artillery. Drunk at Petersburg, Virginia, disturbed a religious meeting by addressing the preacher with filthy language. Cashiered. (LL3119).

Griffiths, C. G. M.
   Contract surgeon. Removed 1/12/64 "by order of the medical director." BL.

Grimes, Lewis.
   Asst. Surgeon. 32nd Ohio. After only three months in service he was dismissed 7/23/64 for straggling, getting captured, and giving information to the enemy. He was re-instated four months later. UW.

Guenste, F.
   Asst. Surgeon. 35th Pennsylvania. Drunk, cursing, broke arrest, at Hunter's Chapel, Virginia. Dismissed. Court suggested clemency. (II607).

Bad Doctors

Haley, George D.
: Asst. Surgeon. 1st Maine Cavalry. Dismissed November 1862. Was a POW at Middleton, VA, in May 1862. Pre-war residence Eastport, ME. Post-war residence: Peabody, MA. RRS.

Hall, Henry M.
: See Special Cases chapter.

Hall, John A.
: A Canadian contract surgeon removed "by order of the surgeon-general [William A. Hammond]." BL.

Hall, Lyman.
: Asst. Surgeon. 63rd Illinois. Sold hospital whiskey to soldiers. Sold hospital flour. The record is in great disarray and incomplete. (LL271).

Hall, Richard R.
: Contract surgeon. Removed 1/23/65 for "neglect of duty." BL.

Hamilton, John F.
: Surgeon. 1st Colorado Cavalry. Stole a box of medicine and two blankets. Acquitted. (LL613).

Hance, Samuel F.
: Surgeon. 89th Illinois. He was accused of refusing to treat men with gonorrhea, and of making them buy their own medicines rather use government-supplied medicine. A ladies committee in Chicago had sent him $100 (worth between $3,000 and $10,000 today) for the care of the sick, a sum which he refused to account for. He was acquitted, but resigned and went home. TS. (LL375).

Hand (?), H.
: Contract surgeon. Removed 6/1/64. "Not to be employed again." BL.

Hand, Sherman Milton.
: Asst. Surgeon. 137th New York. Dismissed March 16, 1863. Commissioned in September 1862 at age 33. Post-war residence: Norwich, NY. RRS.

Hardinge, George.
: At Boone County, Missouri, this civilian doctor was charged with cursing and threatening to kill a US colored soldier. He was sentenced to a year in prison, plus posting a bond and paying a fine. (NN2390).

The Roster

Hardman, Jacob.
   Contract surgeon. Removed 1/14/65 for "professional incapacity." BL.

Harned, J. E.
   Contract surgeon. Removed 2/13/65 for "non-compliance with orders." BL.

Harris, E. H.
   Asst. Surgeon. Regular Army. (Can't find in Heitman. There was a Dr. E. H. Harris in an Iowa regiment). On the hospital steamer *N. W. Thomas* lost barrels of rice, beans, and flour, at New Orleans. Acquitted. (NN2857).

Hassenplug, J. H.
   Contract surgeon. Removed 4/26/65 for "rascality, fraud and embezzlement." He also served as Asst. Surgeon in the 109th Pennsylvania. Lived at 611 N. 10th St., Philadelphia. Died 11/25/1899. BL.

Hastings, David C.
   Asst. Surgeon. 27th Iowa. Refused to go with a guard to protect a forage train. Acquitted. (LL501).

Hayes, Asa H.
   Asst. Surgeon. 16th Wisconsin Veteran Volunteers. Dismissed for disobedience and AWOL. UW.

Haymaker, G. H.
   Contract surgeon. Removed 1/19/64, "not to be employed again." BL.

Hays, John.
   Contract surgeon. Removed 5/6/65 for drunkenness. BL.

Hazen, J. H.
   Contract surgeon. Removed 2/15/65 for "uncourteous behavior and exhibiting strong symptoms of insubordination." BL.

Heaney, Patrick.
   Asst. Surgeon. 5th Pennsylvania Cavalry. At Williamsburg, Virginia, allowed the hospital to run out of medicine. Not his fault. Acquitted. Good description of running a hospital. (NN497).

Bad Doctors

Heath, Charles E.
> Asst. Surgeon. 57th Massachusetts. Dismissed 11/22/64 for tendering his resignation on grounds of disability. His commander said Heath was a "coward and worthless." UW.

Heiland, Charles.
> Asst. Surgeon. 20th New York. Dismissed October 4, 1862, probably for AWOL. Commissioned June 1861 at age 33. RRS.

Henderson, James.
> Asst. Surgeon. 201st Pennsylvania. Drunk at Chambersburg, Gainesville, and Manassas Junction. Stole liquor. Neglected the sick. Dismissed. (NN3034).

Henderson, W.
> Contract surgeon. Removed 3/2/65 for obtaining a pass under false pretenses. BL.

Hereford, James H.
> Surgeon. 39th Kentucky. He was born when Ben Franklin was still alive. Hereford was accused of being "tyrannical and supercilious," incompetent, and out of line for pointing a pistol at another surgeon. Hereford refused admission of men with severe malaria. Hereford was convicted and dismissed. His 1870 pension application was rejected. After threatening witnesses with violence until they backed his story, he finally received a pension. His widow's pension was rejected, but her appeal to President Cleveland was successful and she received money until 1903, based on her husband's flawed service. In 1918, Hereford's daughter launched a vigorous political campaign to receive a Civil War pension herself, but failed. TS. (LL1079).

Herriman, W. L.
> Contract surgeon. Removed 7/18/64 for "incompetence." BL.

Herwig, E.
> Contract surgeon. (Can't find him in *Heitman* or in civilwardata.com.) Threatened to shoot the surgeon at Memphis. Neglected his patients. Dismissed. (LL2677).

Herwig, E.
> Contract surgeon. Removed 10/1/64 for AWOL and misconduct. BL.

The Roster

Hettich, C. F.
　Asst. Surgeon. 108th Ohio. Dismissed 12/9/62, after serving only three months, for "basely deserting the sick and wounded of his regiment during the engagement at Hartsville [Tennessee] on Dec. 7, 1862." UW.

Hewett, James D.
　Surgeon. 119th New York. Dismissed June 14, 1863. He was also Asst. Surgeon, 66th New York. Post-war residence: New York City. RRS.

Hewitt, Thomas.
　Contract surgeon. Removed 11/20/63 for "misconduct." BL.

Hezlep, William B.
　Surgeon. 3rd Pennsylvania Cavalry. He graduated from Philadelphia's Jefferson Medical College in 1854 and ten years later was with the 3rd Pennsylvania Cavalry, where he was court-martialed for being drunk on duty at the battle of New Hope Church, doing amputations. Witnesses agreed he'd been drinking, was probably drunk, but "was not too drunk to operate." Vivid operative story. He was acquitted. He later served in the 6th Pennsylvania Heavy Artillery. TS. (LL1766).

Hicks, Wilson T.
　Asst. Surgeon. 7th West Virginia. Went beyond the picket line. Acquitted. (LL770).

Higgins, John.
　Surgeon. 12th Illinois Cavalry. Sold six government horses and kept the money. Acquitted. (NN2928).

Hills, Thomas Morton.
　Asst. Surgeon. 27th Connecticut. Dismissed February 2, 1863. Post-war: New Haven, CT. Died 1901. Buried Old Windham Cemetery, Windham County, CT. RRS.

Hitchcock, H. O.
　Contract surgeon. Removed 2/8/65 for "grave misdemeanors." BL.

Hoffman, James M.
　Surgeon. 155th Pennsylvania. After six months with his regiment, he was accused of selling whiskey to soldiers who had just completed the freezing misery of Burnside's Mud March, and of eating part of a can of government peaches. The court heard lengthy testimony, reviewed hospital records, and convicted Hoffman,

but suggested mitigation. Joseph Hooker refused the request for clemency. TS. (LL80).

Holbrook, William.
Surgeon. 18th Massachusetts. Did not go into Washington, DC to procure medicine. He had a fractured fibula. Acquitted. (LL1377).

Holden, D.
Contract surgeon. Removed 3/17/65 for drunkenness. BL.

Holden, Duane A.
Contract surgeon. Removed 11/9/64 for drunkenness and neglect of duty. Rehired October 1865. BL.

Holmes, L. E.
Contract surgeon. Rejected by board, date not recorded. BL.

Hood, George H.
Asst. Surgeon. (Not in *Heitman* or civilwardata.com.) Beat and abused a sick man at Westport, Missouri. Dismissed. Restored on a technicality. (NN2210). He was also a contract surgeon, in charge of US General Hospital, Kansas City, Missouri, in 1864.

Hostetler, J. A.
Asst. Surgeon. 116th Illinois. Record is lost. (NN3931).

Hough, F. R.
Surgeon. 97th New York. Ate hospital rations. Shared a meal with the cook. Acquitted. (LL160).

Houston, Joseph M.
Asst. Surgeon. 3rd Delaware. Habitually drunk. Sold hospital floor boards. Fed a noted rebel. Failed to vaccinate his troops. Fined two months pay and reprimanded. (NN1760).

Hovey, B. L.
Surgeon. 136th New York. Wrote a letter to the *Danville Advertiser*, disagreeing with Lincoln's policy on slavery. Record very faded. (LL348).

Howland, Hiram.
Asst. Surgeon. 8th New York. Failed inspection. "I was too busy, the only doctor for two regiments." Fined one month's pay and reprimanded. (LL3125).

The Roster

Hoyt, M. C.
>Surgeon. 1st Congressional District of Wisconsin. He charged many draftees for the induction examination. Fined $300 (roughly $10,000 today) and was dismissed. Maj. Gen. Pope said he should be "disgracefully dismissed" and his crime published in newspapers. Hoyt of course appealed. (NN2762).

Hubbard, George C.
>Surgeon. 165th New York. At Morris Island, South Carolina, he encouraged men not to deliver the colors. He was reprimanded. (MM3007).

Hubbard, S. G. (?)
>Contract surgeon. Removed 4/6/64 for disrespectful language. BL.

Hudson, Abisha.
>Surgeon. 45th Illinois. Case dismissed for lack of quorum. He resigned two months later. (NN3816).

Huebachmann, Francis.
>Surgeon. 20th Wisconsin. In two months, he drank seventy-two bottles of hospital "liquor" and seven gallons of hospital whiskey. He was drunk at Bull Run and Gainesville. He lost (literally) several patients, one of whom has never been found. He insulted most of the officers. He was reprimanded. (KK734).

Hughes, John W.
>Asst. Surgeon. 48th US Colored Troops. Dismissed October 1864. RRS.

Huntoon, Andrew J.
>5th Kansas Cavalry. Dismissed March 20, 1862 at St. Helena, Arkansas. Commissioned January 1862 (lasted two months!) at age 27. Pre- and post-war residence at Topeka, KS. RRS.

Huston, W. C.
>Contract surgeon. Removed 8/16/64. Habitually drunk. BL.

Hutchins, O.
>Contract surgeon. Removed 1/2/65. Habitually drunk. BL.

Hutchinson, Edwin.
>Surgeon. 137th New York. Dismissed 3/27/65 for AWOL and failure to meet commission. Dismissal revoked. UW.

Hutchinson, William F.
Asst. Surgeon. 22nd New York. At Arlington, Virginia, had dinner with a private citizen, while on picket. "I didn't know it was forbidden." Reprimanded. (II732 and II625).

Hutton, George.
Contract surgeon. Removed 10/3/64 for incompetence. BL.

Hyatt, J. S.
This civilian doctor denounced the Union, fired his pistol at one surgeon and vandalized the office of another, whom he called "a black Republican." The case ended in a confusing legal tangle. (KK821).

Irwin, Charles A.
Contract surgeon. Removed 10/4/64 for "failing to comply with orders." BL.

Isham, Nelson.
Asst. Surgeon. 97th New York. Ate with the cook. Stole and ate hospital food. Witness said the doctors got soft, white bread while the patients got hard tack. Isham tried to assert that hard tack was better for sick people. (!) Acquitted. (LL160). Tried a second time, ten months later. He asserted that he had provided herring, cheese, and sausage equivalent to the $75 of hospital food he had eaten. Long discussion of the officer's mess bill. Fined $75 and reprimanded. Reviewing general said the sentence was "much too lenient." (NN559).

Jackson, Eben.
Surgeon. 30th US Colored Troops. At Wilmington, NC, a Union sharpshooter was shot in the chest and was carried through the rain to the camp of the 30th US Colored Troops, arriving around midnight. Jackson did not treat him but said, "Carry him to the hospital." He was tried for "inhumane neglect." Jackson said that in the dark, on the muddy ground, there was no way he could operate. He was ordered dismissed. Many review officers had varying opinions. In the end, he was reprimanded and then resigned. Prior service in the 17th Wisconsin. Died 1898. TS. (MM1664).

Jackson, G. W.
Contract surgeon. Removed 12/22/64 for drunkenness. BL.

The Roster

Jackson, J. A.
Contract surgeon. Removed 1/14/65 for drunkenness. BL.

Jacobs, Ferris.
Surgeon. US Volunteers. Resigned 12/22/62 after eight months service. Died 1887. UW.

Jassay (Jassey), John.
Asst. Surgeon. 124th Illinois. Dismissed for 11/17/64 for "repeated disobedience." UW.

Jeffray, Thomas R.
Surgeon. 9th Kentucky. AWOL two weeks at Knoxville. Surgeon's certificate says he was sick. Acquitted. (LL2578).

Jett, William H.
Surgeon. 26th Kentucky. Drunk twice at Salisbury, North Carolina. Cursed paroled prisoners, thus "outraging every principle of manhood." Challenged a lieutenant to a duel. Dismissed. (MM2407).

Johnson, John D.
Surgeon. US Volunteers. At Chattanooga he was accused of drinking whiskey intended for the patients. The total amount was half a pint. Johnson said the stench of infected wounds was so great that he needed whiskey for his nerves. He was dismissed. But in a death bed confession, his accuser admitted he'd made up the story. On April 26, 1864, Lincoln re-instated Dr. Johnson, following Judge Holt's recommendation. TS. (MM1293 and MM766).

Johnson, William A.
Contract surgeon. Removed 6/16/64 for "disobedience of orders and absence without leave." BL.

Johnson, William P.
Surgeon. 18th Ohio. He was a member of the Ohio state legislature. He tried to resign so he could attend the session. Resignation not approved, so he went on a leave of absence. Returned late with a medical excuse of "bilious colic." Acquitted. (LL2414).

Jones, Caleb V.
Surgeon. 63rd Indiana. At Atlanta, Georgia, abused a patient, refused to visit another sick man, and called the colonel a "damned little whiffet," a breed of small, snappish dog. Dismissed. (LL3002).

Bad Doctors

Jones, William.
   This civilian doctor was arrested for smuggling quinine into the Confederacy via Memphis, but for families, not for the Confederate army. He was convicted and sentenced to take the Oath of Allegiance. (KK285).

Jones, Yearsley.
   Contract surgeon. Removed 3/28/65 for "disobedience of orders and inefficiency." BL.

Jones, Z. Ring.
   Contract surgeon. Removed 1/10/65 for disobedience of orders. He was later commissioned as surgeon in the 195th Pennsylvania Infantry. BL.

Joslin, Eliab M.
   Surgeon. 6th Missouri Infantry. In 1856, he had been president of the National Republican Association. In 1862 he was court-martialed for stealing a case of wine, eight bottles of whiskey, and thirty pounds of candles, as well as being AWOL several days. The liquor and candle issue seemed to be an accounting problem. He was reprimanded for the AWOL and served two more years. By then he was so sick he had to be carried. He died in Orange, California, now a Republican stronghold. TS. (KK487).

Junghanns, Louis H.
   Surgeon. 12th Missouri. He had been with the regiment seven months when he was court-martialed. The charges were that he complained too much about large animals around the hospital, that he was drinking beer with friends when he should have been doctoring, and that he refused to treat the wounded at Vicksburg. He said he was too sick for duty. After long and contradictory testimony, he was convicted, dismissed, and disappears from the record. TS. (LL905).

Keasby, John B.
   Surgeon. District of Columbia Board of Enrollment. Took bribes, enlisted sick men, etc. A huge file. Even Stanton got involved. Dishonorably dismissed. (NN3321).

Keedy, Sam H.
   Contract surgeon. Removed 6/1/65 for "desertion of post." BL.

The Roster

Keeler, Levan J.
   Surgeon. 6th Kentucky Cavalry. Dismissed 8/14/64 for stealing Sanitary Commission whiskey, selling it, and keeping the money. Also sold adulterated whiskey. UW.

Keith, Price.
   Asst. Surgeon. 3rd US Colored Troops. Drunk four months at Memphis. Kept a colored woman in his tent. Many witnesses could hear him with "Sallie." Cashiered. (MM2773).

Kelly, John.
   Contract surgeon. Removed 9/29/65 for drunkenness. BL.

Kemper, G. W.
   Asst. Surgeon. 17th Indiana. Dismissed 7/27/64 for using his veterans furlough and then applying for a discharge. UW.

Kendall, Reece P.
   Surgeon. 7th US Colored Heavy Artillery. Tried to choke the assistant surgeon. Stole hospital rations. Failed to replace louse-filled bedding at Fort Pickering, Tennessee. Acquitted. (OO696).

Kennedy, David.
   Contract surgeon. Removed 11/7/64 for disobedience. BL.

Kerr, George.
   Contract surgeon. Removed 11/7/64 for AWOL. BL.

Kerrigan, Joseph A.
   He was a recruiting medical examiner in New York City, working for the notorious fraudster Brig. Gen. Francis Spinola. Kerrigan "examined" and passed three drunk French sailors from a French warship at anchor in New York Harbor, and "passed" several very unqualified "Negroes." Kerrigan was convicted on several of the charges and sentenced to be "forever disqualified" from being a government doctor. This restriction was later overturned by Kerrigan's political friends. TS. (LL1714).

Keyes (Keys), John W.
   Asst. Surgeon. 133rd Pennsylvania. Dismissed January 28, 1863. RRS.

Kincaid, J. J.
   Contract surgeon. Removed 6/1/63 for drunkenness and neglect of duty. BL.

Bad Doctors

Kirby, Henry.
> Asst. Surgeon. 84th Indiana. AWOL twice near Nashville. Pleaded guilty. "My wife was sick." Reprimanded. (NN82).

Kittridge, Floyer G.
> Surgeon. 31st Massachusetts. He was court-martialed twice for AWOL and was ordered dismissed. The dismissal was sent to Lincoln for review. (Can't find a Lincoln note in Basler or in *Merciful Lincoln*.) Meanwhile, he was court-martialed a third time for a recruiting scandal regarding black soldiers, issuing certificates of health without an actual examination, and extorting money from wealthy blacks. He was acquitted, but heavily censured by the reviewers. TS. (LL850, LL1108, and MM874).

Kleine, Lewis.
> Asst. Surgeon. 90th New York. Deserted at Camp Sheridan, Virginia. Dismissed. Gen. Hancock approved dismissal. (OO351).

Kline, G. H.
> Asst. Surgeon. 37th Pennsylvania. Dismissed March 1, 1863. RRS.

Klueber, Emil H.
> Contract surgeon. Removed 12/21/63 for incompetence. BL.

Knapp, William D.
> Asst. Surgeon. 19th Massachusetts. Dismissed after only nine months of service. UW.

Knickerbocker, Bolivar.
> Asst. Surgeon. US Volunteers. Accused of stealing mackerel, mutton, beef, ham, pork, bread, flour, coffee, butter, ginger, salt, pepper, etc., etc. at Camp Butler, Illinois. Used it to feed the patients, who testified that the food was MUCH better under Dr. Knickerbocker. Acquitted. In 1865, brevetted major for "faithful and meritorious service." Resigned from army 1876. Died 1901. (MM3658).

Knorr, M. K.
> Contract surgeon. Removed 12/31/63 "by order of the medical director." Rehired in May 1864. BL.

Krechbach (?), M.
> Contract surgeon. Removed 11/21/63 for "bad character." BL.

The Roster

Krumsick, August.
Surgeon. 3rd Missouri. Dismissed January 1863. RRS.

Kuhn, H.
Contract surgeon. Removed 1/23/65 for "incompetence." BL.

Lafontaine, Lavis.
Contract surgeon. Removed 4/25/65 for "inefficiency and disobedience of orders." BL.

Laing, James M.
Asst. Surgeon. US Volunteers. As a witness in a court-martial refused to answer questions six times. Acquitted. Brevetted lieutenant colonel in 1865 for "faithful and meritorious service." (NN19).

Lakeman, William H.
Surgeon. He served in the 13th and 76th New York Infantry and was court-martialed three times. He claimed to have been a "dresser" and a "clinical clerk" at St. Thomas Medical College in London, and signed himself "William H. Lakeman, MD." He was tried twice for being drunk as a hospital steward with the 13th New York, and with making many dispensing errors. (A dead leech floating in a bottle of medicine.) Also tried for being drunk during battlefield surgery. After being cashiered and ejected from the service, he was arrested for being drunk in Washington, DC. In the late 1880s he was reported both dead and alive. Did he ever actually hold an MD degree? TS. (KK408 and KK437).

Lamb, David W.
This civilian doctor was convicted of trying bribery to help his $7,000 claim against the government. Convicted. Six months in jail and a $500 fine. (MM3644).

Lamb, J. B.
Surgeon. 35th Missouri. Neglected the sick on the steamboat *Rocket*, on the White River. Acquitted. (LL373).

Lane, Samuel.
Asst. Surgeon. 5th Pennsylvania Reserves. AWOL. He'd been in the army three days. His regiment was out of medicine so he went into Washington, DC, to buy some and was arrested. "I didn't know I needed a pass." Reprimanded. (II659).

Laudon, R. B.
>   Contract surgeon. Removed 9/15/64 "by order of the Surgeon-General." BL.

Lauer, Charles F.
>   Asst. Surgeon. 55th Pennsylvania. Assaulted and tried to rape six different colored women and girls. Outrageous testimony of brutality. Reprimanded and fined two month's pay. See co-author TPL's *Sexual Misbehavior in the Civil War*. (NN624).

Lawrence, Thomas.
>   Asst. Surgeon. 11th Missouri Cavalry. Drunk and rowdy at Brownsville, Arkansas. Acquitted. (OO423).

Lazier, Henry B.
>   Contract surgeon. Removed 1/22/65 for "neglecting to comply with orders." BL.

Le(w?), W. H.
>   Contract surgeon. Removed 11/10/64 for "incompetence and neglect of duty." BL.

Leal, John R.
>   Surgeon. 144th New York. Dismissed 1/4/64, but still with the regiment in June 1865, in spite of not meeting with the commission. UW.

Lee, Charles A.
>   Contract surgeon. Removed 11/13/63 for "neglect of duty." BL.

Lee, J. Hamilton.
>   Surgeon. 21st Connecticut. Left his regiment at Chuckatuk, Virginia and Reed's Ferry, Virginia. (Good battle descriptions). Acquitted. (NN159).

Lee, William D.
>   Contract surgeon. He worked on the POW camp at Camp Douglas, Illinois, where he aided a plot to let a rebel prisoner escape. File has photos and letters to Lincoln. Sentenced to a year in prison, later shortened to six months. (NN1327).

Legler, Henry Theodore.
>   Asst. Surgeon. 8th New York. Dismissed August 27, 1862. On March 27, 1863 he was commissioned into the US Volunteers as a Staff Surgeon and was brevetted major on March 13, 1865

The Roster

for "faithful and meritorious service." Mustered out June 4, 1866. Born in Germany. RRS.

Lehman, Henry.
> Asst. Surgeon. (Can't find in either *Heitman* or civilwardata.com.) At Savannah, Georgia, viciously tortured and killed many "colored" citizens, using pressure hoses, whips, and clubs. Eighty-four pages of testimony. Acquitted. (OO1191).

Lehman, Henry.
> Contract surgeon. Removed 5/23/65 for "incompetence," but rehired in April 1866 for seventeen months. Probably the same Henry Lehman. BL.

Lescher, Samuel P.
> Asst. Surgeon. 100th US Colored Troops. At Murfreesboro, Tennessee, "so drunk he lost all control of himself." At the battle of Decatur, Alabama, left his men with no medical care. Dismissed. (OO1237 and MM26).

Lewis, E. C.
> Contract surgeon. Removed 10/10/63 for disobedience. BL.

Lewis, Robert.
> Contract surgeon. Removed 4/6/64 for incompetence. BL.

Lincoln, T. M.
> Contract surgeon. Removed 6/25/64 for "inefficiency and drunkenness." BL.

Linsley, W. B.
> Contract surgeon. Removed 11/7/64 for "shirking" while treating yellow fever at New Orleans. BL.

Little, David.
> Surgeon. 13th New York. Failed to visit his patients for twelve days at Fort Bennett, Virginia (at Arlington Heights, overlooking the Potomac River). Acquitted. McClellan furious at acquittal. (II614).

Little, George S.
> Asst. Surgeon. 97th New York. At Fletcher's Chapel, Virginia, in a quarrel about who was in charge, assaulted the surgeon. Dismissed. (MM84 and LL312).

Livingston, Allen C.
>Surgeon. 110th New York. Left his regiment at Berwick, Louisiana. He said he had fever and diarrhea. Dismissed. Maj. Gen. Banks remitted the sentence. (LL1095, NN857, and NN1435). As a civilian surgeon, four months later, at Franklin, Louisiana, fraud involving a horse. Guilty. Ten years hard labor. (LL1679).

Long, J. G.
>Asst. Surgeon. 129th Pennsylvania. Dismissed November 26, 1862. RRS.

Maddon, James.
>Asst. Surgeon. 95th New York. Failed to visit the sick for three days. He was sick himself. Acquitted. (NN1938).

Malone, John.
>Surgeon. 71st Pennsylvania. At Falmouth, Virginia accused of fraud involving butter, sausage, chicken, cabbage, pies, ink, and nitric acid. Details about measures and prices. (e. g., a firkin of butter). Cashiered and ordered to make restitution. (KK591).

Man (?), W. H.
>Contract surgeon. Removed 5/6/65 for incompetence. BL.

Marshall, Edward G.
>Asst. Surgeon. 124th New York. Dismissed August 7, 1863. He had prior service with the 71st New York. RRS.

Martin, George.
>Contract surgeon. Removed 1/12/64 "by order of the medical director." BL.

Martin, James.
>Asst. Surgeon. 46th US Colored Troops. AWOL three weeks at Vicksburg, Mississippi. Deserted for six months in Louisiana. Reduced to the ranks, with hard labor in a military prison for the rest of his enlistment. (MM1615).

Maxfield, Kinsey (?).
>Contract surgeon. Removed 1/21/65 "by command of Major General [Cadwallader] Washburn." BL.

The Roster

Maynard, Henry J.
> Surgeon. 1st Arkansas Cavalry. Dismissed for AWOL and re-instated after meeting with commission. Prior service with 59th Illinois, where he was promoted from assistant surgeon. UW.

McCandless, James N.
> Surgeon. 77th Pennsylvania. Tried for cruelty. Taunted sick men. Ordered a sick man to march. The man died. All at Bull's Gap, Tennessee. (Worth an article.) He died at Prescott, Arizona in 1904. (OO987).

McClellan, T. (?).
> Contract surgeon. Rejected by board, date unknown. BL.

McClelland, J. S.
> Contract surgeon. Removed 11/12/64 for "malfeasance in office." BL.

McConaughy, John B.
> Surgeon. 17th Missouri. Dismissed 3/7/64. Re-instated the following month. Prior service in the Missouri Benton Cadets. UW.

McCoy, George.
> Contract surgeon. Removed 11/25/63 "by order of Surgeon [and colonel] Robert O. Abbott." BL.

McCullough, J. R.
> Contract surgeon. Removed 9/17/64 for selling liquor to soldiers Also dismissed from the 82nd New York 2/64. BL.

McCullough, J. R.
> See Special Cases chapter.

McCune, George W.
> Asst. Surgeon. 14th Indiana. Called a captain a "low-flung, low-lived son of a bitch," for having furnished the patients at Bolivar Heights beef "not fit for a dog to eat." Reprimanded. (NN4021).

McCurdy, William F.
> Surgeon. 87th Pennsylvania. Dismissed 2/24/64 for AWOL and failure to appear before commission. UW.

McGregor, T. A.
> Contract surgeon. Removed 9/12/63 for incompetence. BL.

McKinley, S. E.
> Contract surgeon. Removed 11/13/63 for incompetence. BL.

McKinney, D. F.
Contract surgeon. Removed 2/17/65 for "deserting his post." BL.

McKinny, J. W.
Surgeon. 63rd Illinois. AWOL one month from a leave of absence. Acquitted. (NN1937).

McLaurie, Charles M.
Contract surgeon. Removed 5/19/64 for disobedience. BL.

McLetchie, Andrew.
Surgeon. He served with the 79th New York, the "Highland Regiment," a unit with deep Scottish roots. After good work at Bull Run, he ended up working at Camp Parole, where he drunkenly forced his way past a sentry, and at sick call was too drunk to remember what he just asked a patient. The court-marital was marred by intense quibbling by McLetchie's lawyer. McLetchie was convicted and dismissed. Intense political pressure (including the Scottish lobby) pushed Lincoln to remit the sentence. TS. (LL1621).

McMahon, James.
Asst. Surgeon. 54th Kentucky. At Nelson County, Kentucky, shot and killed civilian John O'Brien. Seems that O'Brien was strangling McMahon and trying to bite off the doctor's nose. Many witnesses stated that O'Brien was a notoriously bad man, a drunken brute. McMahon was convicted of murder and sentenced to hang, but was later remitted. (OO1466).

McNutt, Robert.
Asst. Surgeon. 38th Iowa. At Brownsville, Texas, stayed out all night, twenty-six times. Avoided seeing patients. Insulted several officers. Dismissed. (LL2628).

Mears, G. W.
He was a contract surgeon at Murfreesboro, Tennessee. He was sentenced to a year in prison. The trial papers are missing. (NN156).

Meek, John A.
Asst. Surgeon. 89th Indiana. Drunk at Memphis, caused a false arrest. Acquitted. (NN913).

Meeker, Daniel.
>   Surgeon. US Volunteers. He took a nurse to church with him. She had been a prostitute. Took a bribe from a sutler. False certificate of employment for laundresses, all at Camp Nelson, Kentucky, now a Federal cemetery. Acquitted. (OO1102).

Mendenhall, William T.
>   Asst. Surgeon. 57th Indiana. At Murfreesboro, Tennessee he beat up Surgeon John M. Youart, 15th Indiana, while Youart's wife and children were present. He served until 11/63. Dismissed. Later lived in Richmond, Indiana. Dead by 1882. (Worth an article.) (LL525 and LL502).

Miller, James.
>   Contract surgeon. Removed 11/2/64 for drunkenness and AWOL. BL.

Miller, John West.
>   Contract surgeon. Removed 11/26/64 for drunkenness and disloyalty. BL.

Miller, M. M.
>   Contract surgeon. Removed 7/18/64 for disobedience. BL.

Mills, Lucius.
>   Contract surgeon. Removed 11/7/64 for "misconduct." BL.

Millspaugh, Theodore.
>   Asst. Surgeon. 2nd West Virginia Mounted Infantry. AWOL one day. Pleaded guilty. Lost one month's pay. (NN765).

Mitchell, Albert S.
>   Asst. Surgeon. 37th Massachusetts. Dismissed 12/26/63 after nine months of service. Age twenty-three. UW.

Mitchell, George H.
>   Surgeon. 88th Pennsylvania. He created an astonishing record of legal wrangling and self-justification. He went AWOL whenever he felt like it; he got in fist fights; he stole food; he stole building supplies. He was court-martialed three times, was denounced by Lincoln's Judge Advocate General, dismissed by Lincoln, reinstated by the governor of Pennsylvania, etc. etc. After being pardoned by President Hayes, Mitchell demanded back pay. (!)

His widow's 1889 application for a pension was denied. TS. BL. (KK248, KK271 and NN3125).

Montmallin (?), J. M.
   Contract surgeon. Removed 7/29/64 for "disrespectful conduct towards officers commanding colored troops." BL.

Moore, James.
   Asst. Surgeon. 17th Pennsylvania Cavalry. Dismissed 9/5/63. Resigned. Dismissal revoked. UW.

Moore, James.
   Contract surgeon. Date missing. "Nor to be employed again." BL.

Morgan, John A.
   This civilian doctor was convicted of organizing a guerrilla band which shot at steamers on the Mississippi, Arkansas, and White Rivers. Sentenced to hard labor for life, with a ball and chain part of the time. Andrew Johnson remitted the sentence. (NN3773).

Morgan, Thomas L.
   Asst. Surgeon. 10th Missouri. Grossly drunk in a Memphis saloon, attached to the New Theatre. AWOL 19 days at Nashville. Pretended to be Gen. Sherman's chief of staff. Dismissed. (NN2826 and NN213).

Morris, R. N.
   Contract surgeon. Removed 11/14/63 "by order of the surgeon-general." BL.

Morrison, J. B.
   Contract surgeon. Removed 1864 for drunkenness. BL.

Morrison, James M.
   Surgeon. 48th Pennsylvania. In spite of many warnings by his colonel, Morrison got drunk, riotous, and noisy on the streets of Lexington, Kentucky. Dismissed. (NN144 and LL732).

Morrison, W. B.
   Contract surgeon. Removed 12/9/64 for AWOL. BL.

Morrow, Corridon.
   Asst. Surgeon. 43rd Ohio. Dishonorably discharged 2/6/64. Changed to honorable a month later. UW.

The Roster

Moses, Israel.
> Surgeon. US Volunteers. Wrote an insubordinate letter at Murfreesboro, Tennessee. Dismissed. (NN1798). If this is the same Israel Moses described in *Heitman*, he served in the Mexican War, was lieut. colonel of the 72nd New York in 1861, was honorably mustered out in 1862, joined the US Volunteers, and was brevetted lieut. colonel of volunteers in 1865 for "faithful and meritorious service."

Mott, John W.
> Contract surgeon. Removed 2/15/65 for "carelessness and insubordination." BL.

Mulford, Sylvanus.
> Surgeon. 33rd New York. AWOL two days at Alexandria, Virginia. He had "fever." Acquitted. (KK509).

Murray, Henry A.
> Acting Asst. Surgeon. 84th US Colored Troops. He has a brilliant record – up to a point. He had enlisted as a private, was promoted to corporal, sergeant, hospital steward and finally acting assistant surgeon. He was due to be honorably discharged in a few weeks with the 84th USCT. Instead he was arrested dead drunk in three New Orleans whorehouses: 200 Saint Louis Street, Bianca Robinson's house, and Eliza Skinner's house. At his court-martial, Murray was too drunk to stand and was jailed to sober up. Finally awake enough to hear the sentence, he was dismissed. TS. (MM3676).

Nagel, Christopher.
> Asst. Surgeon. 7th New York. Dismissed January 22, 1863, seven days after he was commissioned! He was age 31. RRS.

Neilson (Nielson), Charles F.
> Surgeon. 6th Maryland. Deserted during battle at Winchester, Virginia, rode secretly away and went to Baltimore. He produced a surgeon's certificate: "severe diarrhea." Reviewing general was furious at Neilson's acquittal. (NN5405). In the 1885 index (microfilm 1105) his entry is partly crossed out and very hard to read. NN5405 may be inaccurate.

Nellis, Ozias.
   Asst. Surgeon. 2nd West Virginia Cavalry. Dismissal revoked after meeting with commission. Promoted to surgeon in the 10th West Virginia in 1865. UW.

Nelson, A. A.
   Contract surgeon. Removed 1/25/64 after "unfavorable report of Medical Inspector." BL.

Nelte, Charles.
   Contract surgeon. Removed 10/23/64 for incompetence. BL.

New, George W.
   Surgeon. He was with the 7th Indiana, when he performed the first amputation of the war. (The patient went on to form the nation's premier artificial limb company.) New was accused of selling hospital whiskey. The regiment was moving and had insufficient transport. New sold the whiskey to eager soldiers and used the money to buy hospital supplies at the next stop. He was convicted and dismissed. Lincoln overturned the conviction. New went on to an illustrious career both during and after the war. TS. (II528).

Newhall, Charles H.
   Contract surgeon. Removed 10/25/64 for "unsatisfactory performance." BL.

Newman, George W.
   Asst. Surgeon. 12th Missouri Cavalry. AWOL one month at La Grange, Tennessee. Sick with "chronic diarrhea." Acquitted. (LL2889 and LL2881).

Nichols, Elmer.
   Asst. Surgeon. 118th Illinois Mounted Infantry. Dismissed 7/14/64 for AWOL and failure to meet commission. UW.

Norton, Prior (Pryor).
   Asst. Surgeon. 20th Kentucky. At Louisville, refused to care for sick Confederate POWs. Let men die in prison. (Worth an article.) Reprimanded. (NN2929). In 1868, he obtained his MD degree from the Eclectic Medical College of Cincinnati.

Nugent, John.
   Contract surgeon. Removed 6/14/64 for "inefficiency." BL.

Nugent, R. J. S.
   Contract surgeon. Removed 11/29/64 for drunkenness. BL.

The Roster

O'Connell, Patrick A.
>Surgeon. 28th Massachusetts. Sent a private outside the lines without permission. No prosecution offered. Acquitted. (LL868).

O'Conner, Lawrence J.
>Contract surgeon. Removed 1/4/65 for drunkenness. BL.

O'Donnell, John.
>Asst. Surgeon. 9th US Colored Troops. Dismissed 2/14/4. He deserted after only three months service. UW.

O'Farrell, Gerald.
>Asst. Surgeon. 63rd Pennsylvania. Missed one day of sick call. He'd ridden to the Division Hospital. On his return, the night was very dark and "his horse was blind," so he was delayed. (Totally blind horses cannot be safely ridden.) Witness: "He is a good surgeon." Reprimanded. (LL1606).

O'Neil, James C.
>Asst. Surgeon. 25th New York. Dismissed September 12, 1862. RRS.

O'Shea, Thomas.
>Contract surgeon. Removed 6/22/64 for disobedience. BL.

Oliver, George H.
>Surgeon. US Volunteers. He served as medical director of several camps and hospitals. The governor of Ohio suggested that Oliver was "a drunkard" and should be dismissed. Oliver kept his post. Then the governor of West Virginia called for Oliver's dismissal, for incompetent administration, neglect of patients, and drunkenness. In a rebuttal letter, Oliver described a doctor shortage, efforts to clean the building, and constant diversion from medical duties by interfering visiting politicians. Oliver transferred to New Mexico to help his rheumatism. There he was forced to resign because of drunkenness, but was hired as a contract surgeon in Texas, but there he was considered unfit. His medical officer file has, in huge letters, "BLACK LIST." TS. Both trials are in (NN83).

Orrick, J. W.
>Contract surgeon. Removed 2/1/64 for "dissifration" [sic] BL.

Osborn(e), Nehemiah (Nathaniel).
>Asst. Surgeon. 78th US Colored Troops. Dismissed 3/14/65 for AWOL and failing to appear before commission. UW.

Osborne, J. L.
> Surgeon. 42nd New York. Abandoned his patients at White Oak Swamp and Savage Station. No prosecution offered. Acquitted. (KK86).

Owen, Edward W.
> Asst. Surgeon. 16th New York Heavy Artillery. Stole hospital equipment, shipped it to his wife. He was dishonorably dismissed, to have his crime published in his hometown newspaper, and "it shall be deemed scandalous to associate with him." (NN2923).

Owen, Joshua.
> Surgeon. US Volunteers. Failed to file morning reports of sick patients at Camp Winfield Scott, Virginia. Notes by Jonathan Letterman and Joseph Hooker. Acquitted. Honorably mustered out July 1865. Died 1880. (II836).

Packard, Nelson J.
> Asst. Surgeon. 11th Michigan. AWOL two weeks after a medical leave of absence. He was very "feeble," with "paraplegia." Fined 15 days pay, with a recommendation for clemency. (LL687).

Parker, Clifford.
> Asst. Surgeon. 5th Pennsylvania Cavalry. Dismissed September 30, 1863. RRS.

Parker, Robert.
> Asst. Surgeon. 4th California Infantry. Dismissed 12/5/63. UW.

Parks, Neil O'Donnell.
> Acting Asst. Surgeon (contract surgeon). 32nd US Colored Troops. (Can't find him in *Heitman* or civilwardata.com.) At Hilton Head, South Carolina, stole hospital whiskey, got grossly drunk in front of enlisted men. He said he was treating his malaria with cinchona bark and whiskey. (Rather like gin and tonic, tonic being quinine). Dismissed. Died 1908 at Ashton, Rhode Island. (OO1178 and MM2307.)

Patterson, John J.
> Surgeon. 46th US Colored Troops. AWOL three weeks from sick leave, His steamer, the *Mary E. Forsyth*, was delayed. He had malaria, piles, and debility. Patterson was surgeon-in-chief for the 16th Army Corps. Vicksburg. (LL2776).

The Roster

Patton, R.
> At Chattanooga, this civilian doctor was charged with fraud. He claimed to have 500 gallons of blackberry cordial for sale. Acquitted. (LL2385).

Pease, Loren H.
> Asst. Surgeon. 10th Connecticut. At Portsmouth, North Carolina, sold food, tobacco, ale, and writing paper to patients. Sold counterfeit Confederate money. Danced at a "Negro wedding." Dismissed. (MM809).

Pease, P. C.
> Contract surgeon. Removed 1/25/65 for neglect of duty. BL.

Pease, Philo C.
> Asst. Surgeon. 6th New York. AWOL two days. Acquitted. Good photo in civilwardata.com. (MM1843).

Percy, Henry.
> Asst. Surgeon. (Can't find in *Heitman* or civilwardata.com.) At Camp Nelson, Kentucky, kept a prisoner at the hospital, enabling him to escape. Acquitted. (MM2476).

Perley, J. H.
> Asst. Surgeon. (Can't find in *Heitman* or civilwardata.com.) Used insulting language to a woman who came to the hospital looking for her wounded son. Refused to see Pvt. H. W. Burton who lay dying on the ground with no shelter. Acquitted. (KK548).

Persons, Horace T.
> Surgeon. 1st Wisconsin Cavalry. AWOL from a leave of absence. He had "chronic diarrhea." Acquitted. (22). [a "numbered" court-martial].

Pettinos, James W.
> Surgeon. US Volunteers and 67th Pennsylvania. Extremely drunk on a dozen occasions. Bound and whipped a patient. Falsely proclaimed adultery between his colonel and a Sanitary Commission woman. Litigious. Seven hundred page trial. Lincoln refused to remit. Judge Advocate General Holt writes a proto-feminist brief. (See author's *Merciful Lincoln*, page 41.) Lived at 1918 Christian Street, Philadelphia. (LL2356 and NN2242).

Bad Doctors

Philips, James.
   Contract Surgeon. Ate hospital rations without paying for them. Acquitted. (LL1646).

Phillips, Luther.
   Asst. Surgeon. 14th New York Heavy Artillery. AWOL from a leave of absence at Fort Stedman, Virginia, He was still sick and the roads were blocked by ice. Acquitted. (MM2166).

Phillips, Martin.
   Asst. Surgeon. 22nd US Colored Troops. Dismissed 3/20/65 for AWOL and failure to meet commission. UW.

Pitcher, C. P.
   See Special Cases chapter.

Porter, J. B.
   Surgeon. Regular Army. At Mansion House Hospital, Alexandria, Virginia accused of feeding patients swill and keeping them in chains. "The charges are completely without basis." He served in the army from 1833 through 1862, retired as a major/surgeon, and wrote extensively about medical care in the Mexican War. Died 1869. (II685).

Porter, S. S.
   Contact surgeon. Date unknown. "Inefficiency." BL.

Post, L.
   Contract surgeon. Removed 12/31/63 "By order of the medical director." BL.

Potts, George J.
   Surgeon. 23rd US Colored Troops. The accusations against Potts sound dreadful: mutilating a body, decapitating a corpse, removing organs for practice, "keeping a human head under his bed." The lengthy testimony showed that the cause of death was unknown and Potts was performing an autopsy. The camp was full of stray dogs and the head was in a sack under Potts' bed to keep the dogs from running off with it. In prolonged litigation, Potts was found both guilty and not guilty. Then his regiment was moved to Texas. There they nearly all had scurvy. Potts' plea for vegetables was ignored by the medical higher-ups, but honored by Maj. Gen. Philip Sheridan (!). In this bizarre case, Potts seems to be the hero, not the villain. TS. UW. (MM3067).

Potts, John.
> Asst. Surgeon. 40th Indiana. Drunk on the march. AWOL one night. Cashiered. (KK489).

Prunk, Daniel H.
> Asst. Surgeon. 20th Indiana. Dismissed November 15, 1862. Pre- and post-war residence: Indianapolis, IN. RRS.

Pugsley, Edmond G.
> Asst. Surgeon. 1st Minnesota. Rode a stolen horse at Gettysburg, July 4, 1863, and lied about it. Cashiered. Meade approved sentence. (NN141).

Putnam, Thomas.
> Surgeon. 117th US Colored Troops. Drunk and disorderly on duty "in the field" in Virginia. Cashiered. (MM1528).

Quick, Jacob.
> Surgeon. 22nd New Jersey. Refused to attend a private suffering from a "severe purging of blood," cursed him, told him to wait until morning. Guilty. Fined one months pay. Second trial: cursed and attacked his colonel, and stole meat and potatoes. Acquitted. Both trials in (LL58).

Quidor, John Edwin.
> Surgeon. US Volunteers. Dismissed 12/5/63. Cause not known. Also served in the 2nd New Jersey. UW.

Quinan, Philip A.
> Surgeon. 150th Pennsylvania. Dismissed 12/19/63 after serving seven months. UW.

Quinlan, A. G.
> Contract surgeon. Removed 3/16/65 for "utter worthlessness." BL.

Raiff, B. T.
> Contract surgeon. Removed 11/9/63 "by order of Brig. Gen. [John] Buford." BL.

Ramsay, George M.
> Surgeon. 95th New York. Dismissal revoked 10/23/64 after meeting commission. Mustered out July 1865. UW.

Randall, A. L.
> Contract surgeon. Removal date unclear. "Incompetence." BL.

Ransey, B. F.
   This civilian doctor was charged with being a bushwhacker in Davidson County, Tennessee. Acquitted. (OO1227).

Read, Ezra.
   Surgeon. 21st Indiana. Stole hospital goods at Ship Island, Mississippi, and shipped them to his home, via Adams Express. Acquitted. (LL192 and MM699).

Reed, James A.
   Asst. Surgeon. 69th New York. Dismised March 18, 1863. He was age 45 when commissioned in November 1861. RRS.

Reily, James R.
   Surgeon. 127th Pennsylvania. Failed to visit a dying soldier, who died in his tent without professional attention. When he heard of the death, he took a drink of whiskey and exclaimed, "I hope he's in a better world." [Story is worth a whole article.] The court dismissed the case as "trivial." (KK606).

Reynolds, W. B.
   Contract surgeon. Removed 6/9/65 for "sustaining a Bad Character." BL.

Ribble, James J.
   Asst. Surgeon. 8th New Jersey. Straggled two days on the march to meet the enemy at Mountain Run, Virginia. Acquitted. (NN1605).

Rice, Peter G.
   Surgeon. 7th New York. At Fort Sedgwick, near Petersburg, lay in a bombproof, refusing to attend a wounded lieutenant. Acquitted. (LL2917).

Richards, J. C.
   Contract surgeon. Removed 1/5/64 "by order of the Medical Director." BL.

Richards, William.
   Contract surgeon. Removed 2/7/65 for "personal impropriety (by Brinton)." BL.

Richards, William.
   See Special Cases chapter.

Richardson, M. C. B.
   Contract surgeon. Removed 10/10/64 for disobedience. BL.

The Roster

Richardson, S. G.
   Contract surgeon. Removed 5/17/65 "For the good of the service." BL.

Riley (also spelled Reily), James R.
   Surgeon. 127th Pennsylvania. He was accused of neglecting a Pvt. Britz. After Britz died, Riley took a drink and said, "Here is hoping that Britz is in a better world." The court found the charges unfounded and frivolous. Riley soon transferred to the 179th Pennsylvania, and left no post-war record. TS. (KK606).

Rippey, John M.
   Surgeon. 1st New York Cavalry Veteran Volunteers. AWOL ten days from camp in West Virginia. His paperwork was delayed. Acquitted. (MM1893).

Riss, F. P.
   Surgeon. 52nd New York. He was playing cards with enlisted men, with prizes of wine. One private was his brother. Guilty. Reprimanded. (LL27).

Ritchie, A. J.
   Surgeon. 2nd Indian Brigade. Stole hospital food at Fort Blunt, Cherokee Nation. Acquitted. (NN3804).

Roberts, Marion.
   Surgeon. 3rd North Carolina. Had a deserter as his servant; allowed the deserter to escape. Greenville, Tennessee. Acquitted. (MM2664).

Robinson, David W.
   Surgeon. 40th Iowa. Stole a woman's cook stove at Little Rock, Arkansas. It was very cold and his patients had no clothes. Reprimanded. (OO16 and NN792).

Robinson, John A.
   Asst. Surgeon. 5th New York Veteran Volunteers. AWOL one month from a leave of absence. He had derangement of the kidneys and liver, and an almost-fatal attack of typhoid fever. Acquitted. (OO400).

Robinson, William.
   Surgeon. 8th Kentucky. At McMinnville, he showed up very, very drunk as a family sat down for the mid-day meal. He asked for food. When told that he would be fed after the family ate, he staggered into the yard, urinated in public, and passed out. He

was cashiered. There is no further record. He also served briefly in the 16th Kentucky. TS. (NN115).

Rockwell, P. G.
Contract surgeon. Removed 11/10/64 "by order of the Secretary of War." BL.

Rockwood, Henry.
Asst. Surgeon. 15th Massachusetts. "Conduct unbecoming an officer and a gentleman." His crime? He ate with the hospital attendants. His dismissal was approved by Gen. Meade. (NN229).

Rodenroth, Albert.
Asst. Surgeon. 7th New York. Dismissed July 3, 1865. He was 42-years old when commissioned in September 1864. RRS.

Rogers, Henry I.
Contract surgeon. Removed 9/14/64 for disobedience. BL.

Rolland, H. T.
Contract surgeon. Removed 9/17/64 for incompetence. BL.

Rolls, J. A.
Contract surgeon. Removed 3/2/64 for refusal to appear before a medical examining board. BL.

Root, Joseph P.
Asst. Surgeon. 2nd Kansas Cavalry. The trial record is lost. (NN80).

Ropes, Francis C.
Contract surgeon. Removed 5/18/65 for disobedience. BL.

Rose, Madison H.
Surgeon. 53rd Indiana. At Vicksburg, AWOL two weeks from a leave of absence. Acquitted. (LL1631).

Rosenberger, George.
Contract surgeon. Removed 5/14/64 for "gross carelessness." BL.

Rossvalley, Max L.
Surgeon. 1st Florida Cavalry. Dishonorably discharged December 31, 1864 for refusing to appear before a medical board of examiners. RRS.

The Roster

Rugg, George.
> Asst. Surgeon. 104th New York. At Petersburg, Virginia, wrote a letter denouncing his colonel. Reprimanded, lost 2 month's pay. (NN3094).

Rush, David G.
> Surgeon. 101st Pennsylvania. Dismissed for AWOL. Met commission. Re-instated. January 1865 transferred to US Volunteers. Excellent photo at Library of Congress. UW.

Russell, Edward.
> Asst. Surgeon. 4th Massachusetts Cavalry. Neglected a dying patient for 54 days. Allowed him to lie until his bedsores exposed the bone. Neglected another patient for weeks. Negligent at Hilton Head, South Carolina and at Jacksonville, Florida. Reprimanded. Reviewing general furious at such a lenient sentence. (NN2836).

Rutz, Gallus.
> Asst. Surgeon. 15th Missouri. Dismissed October 1862. Post-war residence: Highland, IL. RRS.

Sabin, Samuel A.
> Surgeon. 9th New York Heavy Artillery. Dismissal revoked 10/17/64 after meeting commission. Discharged on disability January 1865. UW.

Safford, Erasmus.
> Surgeon. 6th West Virginia. At Clarksburg, spoke ill of Gen. Kelly, fed his servant on hospital rations, stole half a peck of pears, told patients that the assistant surgeon prescribed wrong medicine, returned a dozen very sick men to duty, one of whom died. AWOL twelve times. Two hundred page trial. (Worth an article.) Guilty. Fined two months pay and reprimanded. Post-war he was a pension examiner. (NN445).

Safford, Jonas P.
> Surgeon. 73rd Ohio. He was drunk at Cross Keys, Mount Jackson, Woodstock, and Falls Church, all in Virginia. He neglected the wounded. Also took too much opium. Dismissed. (KK634 and KK649).

Salisbury, Samuel T.
> Surgeon. He was on the Board of Enrollment for the Fourth Congressional District of Connecticut. AWOL eight days. Took a bribe to declare a man unfit for service. Removed his brother-in-law's draft notice. Cashiered. $200 fine, two months in prison. (NN567).

Sallman, Ernest.
> Asst. Surgeon. 5th Pennsylvania Cavalry. At Richmond, Virginia, he was so drunk he couldn't leave his tent. Dismissed. (MM1710).

Sanborn, John E.
> Surgeon. 27th Iowa. The trial record is lost. The *Army Register* makes no mention of a dismissal. (MM491).

Sanders (Saunders), John L.
> Asst. Surgeon. 1st Iowa Cavalry. Dismissed 11/10/64 after ten months of service. UW.

Sanger, Simon C.
> Asst. Surgeon. 6th New York Cavalry. Dismissed for the first time in November 1863. Re-instated. Dismissed again for being drunk on a train full of wounded, whom he neglected. UW.

Sattler, Cornelius.
> Asst. Surgeon. 41st New York. He was sent to Washington, DC, to get medical supplies. He returned ten days later – with no supplies. He blamed it on his scurvy. He was reprimanded and lost a month's pay. (LL154).

Sayler, John H.
> Asst. Surgeon. 62nd Ohio. Drunk and disorderly in a whorehouse on Locust Alley, in Richmond, Virginia. Wild testimony. Dismissed. (MM2779).

Schell, Fred A.
> Asst. Surgeon. 71st Indiana. Denounced Lincoln's policies as an "abolition war," stole one hundred pounds of coffee. Acquitted. (NN481).

Schoeckel, Jacob V.
> Surgeon. 45th New York Veteran Volunteers. Stirred up trouble. Told the lieutenant colonel that others were plotting against him. AWOL eight months. At Huff's Saloon, New York City, he boasted

that he would have many officers dismissed. Huge quarrel among Germans. Schoeckel was dismissed. (OO497 and MM246).

Scholl, Erasmus R.
Surgeon. 76th Pennsylvania. Stole rations meant for the sick. Reprimanded. (Worth an article.) (LL15). Post-war was an Examining Surgeon in Reading, PA.

Schulte, John (or Johan).
Asst. Surgeon. 2nd Missouri Artillery. Dismissed March 1862. RRS.

Scott, David.
Asst. Surgeon. 143rd Pennsylvania. Dismissed 4/9/64. Changed to honorable discharge after his resignation. UW.

Scott, William G.
See Special Cases chapter.

Seaman, Marcimus.
Surgeon. 122nd Illinois. Tried twice. First for AWOL. He had chronic diarrhea and rheumatism. Acquitted. (LL586). Second, for drunk on duty. At Parker's Crossroads, Tennessee, he was drunk when the wounded were brought in. Dismissed. (LL586).

Selby, Stephen F.
Asst. Surgeon. 3rd Ohio Cavalry. He was in charge of the hospital for the Contraband (African-American) Camp at Nashville. Seven hundred women and children in tents. Dead bodies unmoved for 48 hours. Shocking conditions. (Worth an article.) Reprimanded and fined two month's pay. (OO904).

Seymour, Frederick.
Surgeon. US Volunteers. A huge file. He kept a woman who was not his wife. He beat her. He knocked the captain down the stairs at Cowan, Tennessee. Dismissed. He appealed to Lincoln. JAG Holt advised against re-instating him. Seymour was born in England, enlisted in 1861 and was booted out in 1864. (NN1210).

Shady, Christian.
Surgeon. 58th Ohio. Neglected the sick at Port Gibson, Mississippi. Failed to prescribe at Vicksburg. Received pay from civilians for treating them with government medicine. Acquitted. (OO481).

Sharpe, Redford.
> Surgeon. 15th New Jersey. The captain found a woman in the ambulance. Sharpe asserted that when a surgeon called for an ambulance that he could do whatever he wanted with it. Reprimanded. (LL237).

Shaw, Albert T.
> Surgeon. 6th Iowa. His wife ran a boarding house at Syracuse, Missouri, fed the boarders with food that Albert stole from the government. Drank hospital whiskey. At Shiloh, left his post, went to the enemy. Acquitted. Missing since December 31, 1864. (KK335).

Shields, Isaac.
> Surgeon. 1st Delaware Cavalry. At Harpers Ferry, West Virginia, stole 400 pounds of white sugar, 584 hats, 144 ounces of Buchu extract, 39 ounces of quinine, 960 opium pills, and other government supplies. [Buchu is still in use as a treatment for urinary tract infections.] Cashiered. (MM2317).

Sickler, Peter E.
> Asst. Surgeon. 10th New York Cavalry. Dismissed 12/5/64 for AWOL. He also had service in the 18th New York, the 48th New York, and the 8th New York Cavalry. He was fatally wounded at Petersburg seven days before Robert E. Lee's surrender. UW.

Siddall, James P.
> Asst. Surgeon. 22nd Indiana. Dismissed 2/16/65 for AWOL and disobedience. Dismissal later revoked. UW.

Silcox, Edwin F.
> Asst. Surgeon. 18th Massachusetts. Dismissed January 6, 1863. Commissioned August 1862 at age 28. Pre-war residence: Springfield, MA. RRS.

Simpson, Frederick.
> Asst. Surgeon. 72nd New York. Dismissed May 9, 1864. Commissioned in September 1861 at age 27. Also served with the 74th New York (74th service not in *Army Register*.) RRS.

Simpson, G. B. F.
> Contract surgeon. Removed 12/17/65 for desertion. BL.

Sisson, Nelson B.
> Asst. Surgeon. 92nd Ohio. Gave improper leave of absence forms. Colonel testified that the surgeons were overwhelmed with

The Roster

measles, typhus, and diarrhea. Over half the regiment was sick. Acquitted. (LL419).

Sloan, Robert J.
Contract surgeon. Removed 10/12/65 for "inefficiency." BL.

Small, Robert.
Contract surgeon. Removed 11/30/64 "continued drunkenness." BL.

Smanders (?), William H.
Contract surgeon. Removed 3/3/65 "at the request of Major General Hooker for bribes." BL.

Smith, Charles J.
Asst. Surgeon. 69th Pennsylvania Veteran Volunteers. Refused to leave the major's quarters when asked to do so. Didn't visit a sick soldier. Entertained enlisted men in his quarters. Cursed other officers. Acquitted. Gen. Gibbons furious at acquittal. (NN3313).

Smith, Frank A.
Surgeon. 148th Illinois. At Tullahoma, Tennessee, May 1865, called a general a tyrant and said, "Hell is too good for that man." Said sick men were not really sick. Reprimand. (MM2891).

Smith, J. H.
Contract surgeon. Removed 12/16/64 for drunkenness and worthlessness. BL.

Smith, J. K.
Contract surgeon. Removed 7/16/64 for "incompetence and neglect of duty." BL.

Smith, James Washington.
This civilian doctor was convicted of helping soldiers of the 71st Ohio to desert to the rebel army. Smith was a surgeon with the Tennessee River Cavalry, a rebel unit. Sentenced to military prison to the end of the war. His ornate gravestone may be seen in the Dover, Tennessee, cemetery. (LL491).

Smith, Jonathan.
Contract surgeon. Removed 12/5/63 for incompetence. BL.

Smith, S. C.
Contract surgeon. Removed 3/10/65 for "constant drunkenness." BL.

Smith, W. R.
> Contract surgeon. Removed 4/28/65 for drunkenness. BL.

Smith, William H.
> Surgeon. 23rd Wisconsin. Forced a drafted man to pay for a medical discharge. Acquitted. (KK549).

Smith, William O.
> Contract surgeon. Removed 1/17/65. "Collusion with the rebels at Elmira, [POW camp] New York." BL.

Smyth, Gonzalvo C.
> Surgeon. 43rd Indiana. File is so large that we couldn't find the actual charges. Seemed to have something to do with being drunk in a whorehouse. Guilty. Cashiered and fined $1,000 (a huge sum today.) (OO1189).

Snorr, Charles W.
> Contract surgeon. Removed 5/18/65 for disobedience. BL.

Snow, George W.
> Asst. Surgeon. 28th Massachusetts. AWOL ten days with a dental problem. Convicted, reduced to the ranks, then re-instated, with a reprimand. (LL708).

Soellig (?), Robert.
> Contract surgeon. Removed 7/26/64 by order of the acting surgeon-general. BL.

Soule, William.
> Surgeon. 21st Connecticut. He was accused of "neglect of duty," in that he had failed to treat a man who was violently coughing up blood, failed to examine a man "helpless with fever," failed to visit a dying sergeant, and failed to examine a man with a broken collar bone. He defended all these actions. An older doctor told the court that salt water was an approved remedy for coughing up blood. Soule was acquitted. Two months later, he resigned. On the back of the letter of resignation, an unknown hand wrote, "Surgeon Soule's usefulness is much impaired by reason of difficulties with the officers of the regiment." TS. (KK594).

Spencer, John A.
> Surgeon. 69th New York. He had only one ambulance. The paymaster wanted to take it convey money to Fairfax Courthouse. Spencer refused. Medical property is surveyed as broken and worn out (Feb. 1864). Reprimanded. (LL1496).

The Roster

Spies, George A.
Surgeon. 47th Ohio. Accused of neglecting his patients and letting them lie in filth. Apparent shortage of clothes and medicine. He was acquitted. The court opined that Spies was the victim of "malicious and unfounded" accusations. He also served in the 106th Ohio. Cannot locate him post-war. TS. (II856).

Steckel, Edmund F.
Asst. Surgeon. 203rd Pennsylvania. At Fort Fisher, North Carolina, failed to attend the wounded. Slept with the untreated wounded. "I was tired." Dismissed. Gen. Schofield said he should be <u>dishonorably</u> dismissed. (MM1954).

Steele, Albert F.
Surgeon. 176th New York. Dismissed 10/14/64 for AWOL. UW.

Steiger, Emil.
Asst. Surgeon. 39th New York. Fraud regarding a $200 horse at Gettysburg. Colonel testified, "The old 39th was full of swindlers." Acquitted. (MM2414).

Stein, Charles.
Surgeon. 58th New York. Dismissed 12/19/63. Re-instated February 1864. Mustered out October 1865 at Nashville. UW.

Stephens, W. M.
Contract surgeon. Removed 5/4/65 for taking government property for his own use. BL. See also court-martial.

Stephens, W. M.
He was a contract surgeon at Island No. 102, Mississippi, where he was charged with stealing a mule, two cows, a calf, two cans of pineapple, 200 pounds of meat, three pounds of sugar, fifteen bottles of whiskey, and a bottle of quinine. He was fined $1,000. (OO1068).

Stephenson, Benjamin.
Surgeon. 14th Illinois. Guilty of AWOL. Punishment unknown. His wife becomes insane with each pregnancy. "It is hereditary in her family. I saw her through her confinement (childbirth) and then returned." (KK471).

Stewart, J. A.
Contract surgeon. Removed 3/24/65 "for the good of the service." BL.

Stocker, Anthony E.
  Brigade Surgeon, was tried for failing to transport the wounded from Fredericksburg to Washington, DC. His six ambulances were stuck in the mud. The paperwork and testimony are very vague and contradictory, even incoherent. He was reprimanded and returned to duty. Died 1897. TS. (II914). As surgeon of US Volunteers he was accused of pricking a patient with a sword, of cursing and pulling the beard of another patient and with "illegal punishments" on sixteen other patients. Acquitted. (NN3787).

Stover, Samuel T.
  Asst. Surgeon. 99th Ohio. Dismissed 4/12/64 after thirteen months of service. UW.

Styer, Charles.
  Surgeon. 99th Pennsylvania. Dismissed in May or March 1863. Previous service as asst. surgeon in the 45th and 179th Pennsylvania. Subsequent service in Regular Army October 1867 to June 1878. Residence post-war: in Philadelphia. Died July 6, 1896. RRS.

Sullivan J.
  Contract surgeon. Removed 1/19/65 for neglect of duty. BL.

Sullivan, John Heron.
  Asst. Surgeon. 3rd New York. Dismissed 5/17/65 for drunkenness. He had previously been ejected from the US Volunteers for drunkenness, with a "do not rehire" notice, which was ignored. Born in Ireland. UW.

Suydam, Charles H.
  Surgeon. 34th New Jersey. Stupified on opium and whiskey for five months, in Kentucky. Took "the pledge" but violated it. Sold hospital rations. (Worth an article.) Acquitted. He also served in the 27th New Jersey. (OO468).

Swain, Enos.
  Surgeon. 5th Kentucky. AWOL ten weeks from a leave of absence. He had "subacute rheumatism." Acquitted. (NN2062).

Swingley, Frederick.
  See Special Cases chapter.

Taft, Harvey S.
  Asst. Surgeon. 105th Ohio. Dismissed 1/18/64. Had previous service in the Missouri Home Guards. UW.

The Roster

Taggart, J. P.
Contract surgeon. Removed 10/31/63 by order of Gen. Hurlburt. BL.

Tammage, Henry.
Surgeon. 34th Kentucky. Dismissed 3/7/64. Re-instated after acquittal. Prior service in the 7th Kentucky. UW.

Tanner, William H.
Surgeon. 176th New York. Dismissed 11/22/64 for AWOL. Prior service in 47th New York and the 148th New York (Burnside Rifles). UW.

Taplin, W. T.
Contract surgeon. Removed 8/16/64 for "disobedience of orders and gross neglect of duty." BL.

Tarrey, C. W.
Contract surgeon. Removed 6/26/64 for "unfitness." BL.

Tauszky, Rudolph.
Asst. Surgeon. US Volunteers. (Born in Hungary). In New Mexico, disobeyed various orders sending him to Fort Craig and to Fort McRae. Breached arrest by leaving his tent to go to the latrine. Dismissed, yet *Heitman* says he was honorably mustered out in July 1865. (LL2668).

Teal, Norman.
Asst. Surgeon. 88th Indiana. AWOL on the march to Savannah, Georgia. A paperwork error. He wasn't AWOL at all. Acquitted. (MM2415).

Thayer, Benjamin F.
Asst. Surgeon. 7th Missouri. At three different battles in Mississippi he either hid or refused to go forward. Told lies about officers and whiskey. Acquitted. (NN1240).

Thayer, William H.
Surgeon. 14th New Hampshire. Court-martialed September 1863 for false food certificates. Acquitted but dismissed at request of reviewing general. Then re-instated. Died 1897. Photo at UW. (MM1128).

Thomain, Robert.
> Asst. Surgeon. 41st New York. Neglected a sick patient. AWOL at Paris, Virginia. Removed a sick man from the ambulance. Threatened another surgeon. Acquitted. (KK323).

Thomas, Luther G.
> Surgeon. 26th New Jersey. At White Oak Church, Virginia, he was tried for being drunk at the Battle of Fredericksburg and letting his patients starve and freeze to death. It appeared that the supply officers ignored his requests for food and blankets. He had 300 patients in a barn. Hospital workers said they never saw him drunk. The court cashiered him, but the review general and Lincoln remitted the sentence. Long note by JAG Holt. Thomas died in 1864. TS. (KK682).

Thomas, Simon.
> Asst. Surgeon. 6th US Colored Heavy Artillery. Drunk at Vidalia, Louisiana. Drank with enlisted men. Court seemed especially upset that he had played the guitar at a "colored people's" dance. Dishonorably dismissed. (MM2576).

Thomas, T. C.
> Asst. Surgeon. 91st Pennsylvania. Dismissed May 14, 1863. RRS.

Thompson, James.
> Surgeon. 4th US Colored Heavy Artillery. He refused to examine a recruit. "I was very busy and not under the command of the colonel who ordered me to do so." Acquitted. (The first question put to Thompson by the court was "Do you believe Jesus Christ to be the Son of God or do you think he was an ordinary good man and not divine?") (MM2636).

Thompson, John H.
> Surgeon. 124th New York. At Petersburg he made a flag of truce and offered to surrender. Told Union troops not to fire at the approaching enemy because he (Thompson) didn't want to get hurt. Cashiered. His name and crime to be published in his two hometown newspapers. He'd fought at Chancellorsville, Gettysburg, and Locust Grove. (LL2736).

Thompson, Thomas.
> Contract surgeon. Removed 4/29/64 for "incompetence." BL.

The Roster

Thorpe, James C.
 Asst. Surgeon. 9th Ohio Cavalry. Dismissed 4/18/64 after six months service. UW.

Tobey, Samuel D.
 Asst. Surgeon. 8th Michigan Cavalry. Drunk on the streets of Pulaski, Tennessee. Acquitted. (MM1537).

Towar, George W.
 Asst. Surgeon. 24th Michigan. AWOL three weeks. He went home to see his very sick brother. Pleaded guilty. Fined seven day's pay. (OO944).

Towner, William D.
 Asst. Surgeon. 158th New York. Drunk at Big Swift Creek, North Carolina, wild, combative. He'd never been drunk before. Ordered dismissed, with a plea for clemency, which was not granted. (MM756).

Treadwell, Joshua B.
 Surgeon. 45th Massachusetts. Age 24. Received bribes for making medical discharges. Case dismissed – he was no longer in the army. Also served in the 62nd Massachusetts. (OO279).

Trenor, John.
 Asst. Surgeon. 2nd New York Cavalry. Court-martialed twice. AWOL 24 hours at Arlington, Virginia. Reprimanded. AWOL three days while under marching orders. (Wife was sick). Reprimanded with loss of two month's pay. (II782 and II812).

Tuck, Cyrus D.
 Asst. Surgeon. 9th Maine. Charged Negro laborers a medical fee at Fernandina, Florida, for care supposed to be free. Stole hospital rations. Sold liquor to enlisted men. Sold government milk and pies to enlisted men. Threatened to "kick the captain's ass." Dismissed. Governor of Maine asks for clemency. Tuck protested and appealed. (KK259).

Ullman, Ludwig.
 Surgeon. Possibly a contract surgeon. (Not in *Heitman*.) Took bribes for medical exams and sick leaves. Discharged. One year in prison, never to hold a job in Federal service, forever. Died 1910 at Springfield, Missouri. (MM316).

Upjohn, William.
   Surgeon. 7th Michigan Cavalry. Dismissal revoked 2/20/65 after meeting commission. He was 56 that year. His nephew founded Upjohn Pharmaceuticals. UW.

Vaill, Charles W.
   Contract surgeon. Removed 5/7/64 for drunkenness. BL.

Van Hummel, Q.
   Contract surgeon. Removed 2/13/65 for neglect. BL.

Van Ingen, James L.
   Surgeon. 5th New York. He was court-martialed twice. He had assaulted a patient, who he thought was talking to a "lewd woman," had taken an orderly (without authorization) to carry his sword, had bashed a secessionist with a chair, and had tendered his card to a lady, unasked, an insult in Victorian etiquette. He also refused to meet with a medical board that was appointed to review his credentials. He soon created such a tangle of litigation that Abraham Lincoln was called upon to clarify the mess. 1868, still complaining. TS. (II700).

Van Vorhis, Flavius J.
   Asst. Surgeon. 86th Indiana. At Nashville, Tennessee he attempted to obtain free admission to Duffield's Theatre by claiming he was a policeman. Acquitted. (NN510).

Van Winkle, Mark.
   Contract surgeon. Removed 6/24/64 for AWOL. BL.

Vertrees, Samuel W.
   Asst. Surgeon. 98th Illinois. Dishonorably discharged May 24, 1863 for theft. Pre- and post-war residence: Louisville, IL. RRS.

Vervais, Joseph A.
   Asst. Surgeon. 2nd Minnesota Cavalry. Dismissed 11/15/64 for AWOL, gross disobedience, and "general inefficiency." Prior service in the 5th Minnesota. UW.

Walker, George S.
   Surgeon. 6th Missouri. Stole hospital stores at Memphis, Tennessee. Acquitted. (NN2059).

The Roster

Warren, Francis G.
>Asst. Surgeon. 5th Maine. Refused to hear an order at Camp Franklin, Virginia. Acquitted. (NN3995).

Waterbury, Robert L.
>Surgeon. 93rd New York National Guard. Drunk at Relay House, Maryland, threw an assistant surgeon out of the barracks, injuring him. Bolted the hospital door. Dismissed. (LL2609).

Waterman, Luther D.
>Surgeon. 8th Indiana Cavalry (same as 39th Indiana Infantry.) AWOL ten days from a leave of absence. Acquitted. "Chronic diarrhea." (LL1187).

Watson, Francis W.
>Surgeon. 18th Illinois. Shared a mess (eating group) with hospital nurses at Little Rock, Arkansas. Stole onions and potatoes from Sanitary Commission stores. Acquitted. (OO1329).

Watts, William.
>Asst. Surgeon. 5th Illinois Cavalry. Drunk at Haines Bluff, Mississippi, for nine days. Drunk for two days at Black River, Mississippi. Acquitted. (OO111).

Webster, Warren.
>Asst. Surgeon. Regular Army. Webster had experience in the frontier Indian wars. His most heated experience was in a New York hospital. One of his patients was a badly wounded man, also wanted for desertion. Webster defied an order which would have arrested his patient and sent him to prison. In Webster's opinion, the man was far too sick for prison life. The issues were territoriality and authority. The doctor was court-martialed for disobedience, convicted, and sentenced to house arrest in his own hospital. Reviewing authorities noted his skill and high reputation as a doctor and shortened the arrest period. TS. (LL1176).

Weidenbach, Augustus.
>Surgeon. 37th Ohio. Dismissed 3/28/64 after five months of service. Failed to meet commission. UW.

Weiler, Ernst.
>Surgeon. 52nd New York. Dismissed 2/6/64 after three months service. Failed to meet commission. UW.

Wellons, Granville S.
> Asst. Surgeon. 91st Ohio. Dismissal revoked after meeting commission in September 1864. UW.

Wheeler, Albert P.
> Surgeon. 6th West Virginia. Dismissed May 5, 1862. RRS.

White, Frank.
> Asst. Surgeon. 31st US Colored Troops. Dismissed 3/27/65 for AWOL and failure to meet commission. UW.

Wight, Charles M.
> Surgeon. 32nd US Colored Troops. Forged three disability certificates. Ran away at two battles in South Carolina: Honey Hill and Deveaux's Neck. Drunk at Honey Hill. Stole liquor. Fed his family hospital food. Huge file, many exhibits. Cashiered and dishonorably dismissed. 1867 still appealing. (MM3352).

Wilber, George D.
> Asst. Surgeon. 5th Wisconsin. At Camp Griffin, Virginia, refused a patient who needed treatment. Failed to make reports. Made a false report. Disrespected Dr. Castleman. Worth a paper. Acquitted. (KK500).

Wilkins, Henry H.
> Asst. Surgeon. 53rd US Colored Troops. Dismissed March 14, 1864. RRS.

Williams, Anderson L.
> Asst. Surgeon. 74th Ohio. AWOL. He accompanied a sick surgeon who had typhoid and pneumonia. His report back to the regiment was captured by guerrillas. Many certificates in file. Acquitted but dismissed. UW. (LL1179 and LL1183).

Williams, Thomas.
> Surgeon. 6th Tennessee Cavalry. Stole $1,000 left in trust by a dying soldier. (Roughly $50,000 today). Even when ordered to give the money to the soldier's heirs by Gen. Washburn, refused. Dismissed, ordered to pay $1,000 to the soldiers heirs. (OO1236).

Willoughby, Henry W.
> Asst. Surgeon. 1st US Colored Troops. Mustered out August 1864 because of "intemperate use of whiskey and opium." UW.

Wilson, Alexander M.
> Asst. Surgeon. 121st Pennsylvania. Dismissed August 7, 1863. RRS.

The Roster

Wilson, Hugh McGregor.
> Asst. Surgeon. 2nd New York Mounted Rifles. Dismissal revoked after meeting with commission. UW.

Wilson, Torrey.
> 2nd Asst. Surgeon. 3rd Wisconsin. Dismissed July 15, 1863. Pre-war residence: Fox Lake, WI. Post-war: Good Thunder, MN. RRS.

Wiser, William H.
> Asst. Surgeon. 2nd New York Heavy Artillery. Age 51 in 1861. Dismissal revoked after he resigned. UW.

Wixam, Isaac.
> Surgeon. 16th Michigan. Stole rations, whiskey, and brandy at Antietam and Falmouth, Virginia. Dismissed, fined $150. Joshua Lawrence Chamberlain was on the court-martial board. Gen. Hooker approved sentence. (LL238 and LL244).

Wolf, Frederick.
> Surgeon. 39th New York. Spread lies about the colonel, at Stevensburg, Virginia. Acquitted. (LL1824).

Wood, George T.
> Asst. Surgeon. 99th Ohio. Dismissed October 1862. RRS.

Woodmanser, Charles S.
> Asst. Surgeon. 120th Illinois. At Memphis, Tennessee, kept a mulatto woman in his room, had intercourse with her. Dismissed. (OO1226).

Woodward, Charles.
> Asst. Surgeon. 26th Illinois. Did not visit the sick. Allowed the hospital to become filthy. Did not use sanitary stores. Used patient's goods for himself. Said, "Lincoln is trying to place a degraded race on equality with a superior race." Spoke well of the Confederacy. Severe reprimand and fined $60. Review general furious at light sentence. (LL299). Tried again on similar charges. (NN3823). Reprimanded again.

Woodward, William.
> Surgeon. 58th Illinois. Acquitted of charging for medicine for a "private disease." He just used the money to buy medicine in town when the army supply was exhausted. The patient with VD was merely reimbursing the doctor. Convicted of refusing to treat

a colored soldier. "I am not here to doctor niggers." Reprimand. (MM2588).

Wright, Charles O.
Asst. Surgeon. 35th Ohio. AWOL twelve days en route to Chattanooga. He was sick. Acquitted. (NN1367).

Wright, William M.
Surgeon. 79th Pennsylvania. Stole a government horse at Chickamauga, Georgia. Refused to return it. Dismissed, fined a month's pay. (OO118).

Wynkoop, Alfred.
Surgeon. US Volunteers. Told troop movements to an enemy sympathizer. Dismissed but remitted June 18, 1863 by Lincoln. Brevetted lieutenant colonel in 1865 for "faithful service." (MM575).

York, William H.
Asst. Surgeon. 15th US Colored Troops. At age twenty-four he passed the examining board for the rank of "Assistant Surgeon for Colored Troops," and was assigned to the 15th US Colored Troops, which had not had a surgeon for a year. Their hopes for a useful doctor were disappointed. He spent much of his time drunk in a nearby whorehouse, where he prescribed for the inmates. Prostitutes testified. (Worth an article.) His brother, lieutenant colonel of the same regiment, testified that William had never been away from home before and was easily led astray. Dr. York was cashiered after six months "service." TS. (MM3483).

Chapter Two
Special Cases

All our misbehaving surgeons generated records, some sparse, some extensive. We present here a sample of ten surgeons, notable both for their activities and for the extensive documentation contained in the records. They illustrate the complexity and difficulty of providing quality medical care in a time of improvisation, confusion, and shortages.

Henry M. Hall, a resident of Danby, Vermont, signed his first contract with the medical corps on April 3, 1862. He was appointed Acting Assistant Surgeon, a non-commissioned rank and was to receive $100 each month. The document was counter-signed by Surgeon General Clement Finley, himself soon to be forced into an unwanted early retirement. Hall served seven months, mostly at Chesapeake Hospital, Hampton, Virginia, and then received a second contract, in December 1862, assigning him to the Army of the Potomac. Over the next twelve months he moved frequently, appearing with different artillery and cavalry brigades, and with the 11th US Infantry, then at Falmouth, Virginia. Were these many moves a reflection of "transferring out" troublesome personnel?

In January 1864 he received a coveted commission, as assistant surgeon in the 23rd US Colored Troops, where he served nine months. He was then promoted to the rank of surgeon (apparently without the customary examination) and assigned to the 41st US Colored Troops, which instantly raised a storm of protest. E. (Eben?) Jackson, Surgeon in Chief, 1st Brigade, 2nd Division, 9th Army Corps, wrote, "This appointment has created great dissatisfaction and general surprise amongst the medical

Bad Doctors

officers." [The] medical officers throughout the Division know that … he is an incompetent person and totally unfit for Assistant Surgeon." Jackson urged cancellation of the transfer and appearance before a board of medical examiners. Three other doctors endorsed these views, one adding that Hall's incompetence had killed a patient. Hall's service with his new regiment ended on October 11, 1864, two weeks after it began. A few days later he received a fourth appointment as a contract surgeon, which lasted until July 30, 1865, when he was unceremoniously booted out.

In April 1865 the Confederate capital, Richmond, Virginia, fell to Union forces. That same month, Hall was put in charge of Richmond's Smallpox Hospital. In June, we find him at Richmond's Howard Grove Hospital, and later at the Almshouse, a stately building, still standing, on the north side of Shockoe Cemetery. There, Hall's career truly came to grief.

With the Confederacy evaporated and civil government not yet reconstituted, in the summer of 1865 law and order was provided by the Union army, acting as provost guard. On July 29th, Hall's career began to unravel quickly. Lieut. Col. John McEntee, 80th New York, Provost Judge, wrote to Surgeon Robert Loughran, Chief Medical Officer, District of Henrico. "I was informed by my clerk, who is an enlisted man, that on Sunday last he was permitted by Dr. Hall the surgeon in charge of Alms House [sic] to have illicit intercourse with one of the lewd women confined at that place for treatment. I deem it my duty as an officer to make this report known to you in order that you may investigate the character of said Dr. Hall. I have heard other reports of the man which cause me to believe that the above statement is true."

Forty-eight hours later, Loughran wrote to Col. J. Simons, Medical Director, Department of Virginia, detailing his investigation. Loughran had interviewed both patients and staff at the Almshouse, who reported that as many as four days would pass before Hall would visit patients and that at least one died of neglect. Further, "… he makes a practice of cohabiting with the patients under his charge many of whom are lewd women of the town, and inmates of the Alms House under treatment for <u>Venereal disease</u>. [Emphasis in the original]. Two sisters complained that their sibling's chief disabilities were from "frequent personal connection" with Dr. Hall. "There are many minor complaints against him all

Special Cases

going to demonstrate his unfitness for his present position or professional association." Loughran recommended dismissal. That same day, Col. Simons wrote to Hall. "Sir – I have to inform you that your contract is annulled this day. You will settle your accounts immediately, send your contract to this office, and leave the Department within three (3) days." Hall was finished. Or was he?

He denounced all the reports as part of a plot against him by members of the 80th New York, and demanded a thorough investigation. "I ask that some Gentleman may be detailed to hear my explanation of the affair and also examine the charges and then if in his opinion a public investigation is required, he can so report." The adage, "Be careful what you wish for, because you might get it," was especially relevant in Hall's case. Capt. Nicholas Hoysredt, 80th New York, was ordered to make the suggested investigation. On August 4th, he submitted a 1,300-word report to Col. McEntee. We cite here only the most salient points.

Mrs. Catherine Blankenship (a woman with a long history of arrests for prostitution) who had been an inmate at the Almshouse for a month, said that Hall frequently had "carnal communication" with young Lizzie Fletcher, that such was against the wishes of Lizzie, and that Hall's attentions had caused much of Lizzie's sickness. Mrs. Blankenship further asserted that Hall's "unusually large private organs" had left Lizzie's "private parts inflamed." (All this seems second-hand information, legally just hearsay.) She went on to describe an argument, in which Hall insisted that Lizzie was having a miscarriage and Catherine thought not. "The deponent has been accustomed to nursing and taking care of sick, and has had considerable practice in the duties of a midwife." (Other records show Blankenship's arrests were mainly for running a whorehouse, which most likely involved a bit of amateur gynecology.) Hoysredt then interviewed Lizzie, who was too sick for extended conversation. He read Blankenship's deposition to her and she swore under oath that such was an accurate narration. The next interviewee was Mrs. Mary Matthews, another Almshouse inmate who shared a room with Mrs. Martha McCullock. One night about ten o'clock, Dr. Hall came to their room. Matthews was partly undressed, lying on her bed (Richmond in July is hot and humid.) McCullock was undressed and lying on a pallet. Hall first lay next to Matthews, then "…he arose from the bed and going to the pallet and … commenced making efforts to have carnal intercourse with her [McCullock]." After screaming and struggling, McCullock was about to yield when Matthews jumped on him. He then threw Matthews on the pallet and tried to rape her. After a two-hour struggle, he left, unsatisfied. The women did not cry out, because they were afraid of him.

An additional witness, Pvt. G. C. Morgan, Co. F, 80th New York, testified under oath. He had been Hall's clerk at the Almshouse. Morgan said the patients spoke constantly of being neglected by Dr. Hall. A patient named Pierce, suffering from severe dysentery, was not visited by Hall for the five days before his death.

Hall denounced the investigation, saying that the 80th New York and lewd women were conspiring against him. He refused to meet with further investigators or with a medical board. The final note in his record is dated 1881. Someone seeking Hall's current address was told "Cedar Falls, Iowa." The Iowa Board of Medicine has no record of him, nor does he appear in the 1880 Iowa census. BL.

William Richards, of "Iowa City, in the State of Iowa," entered the Federal records on February 1, 1863, when he signed up to be a contract physician. The document, completed at Memphis, Tennessee, had the usual pre-printed provisions: he would be paid $100 per month, increased to $113 when performing service in the field, and would provide his own "sets of trephining, amputating, and pocket instruments." He was assigned to the Memphis Smallpox Hospital. It didn't take him long to get in trouble.

On May 16, 1863, he wrote to the surgeon in charge. "Sir: Yesterday about 6 ½ o'clock P.M. I was on duty when I was assaulted by two men of the Hospital one belonged to the Kitchen & the other to the guard. The man from the guard knocked me on the head with a heavy stick & insulted me very badly. It has made me quite sick. The blow on my head nearly knocked me down." A preliminary investigation that same day concluded that "... Dr. Richards provoked the assault, he being under the influence of liquor … I am not in favor of employees insulting officers."

On May 19, a longer report was submitted by Bernard J. Irwin, Superintendent of General Hospitals at Memphis. (Irwin was brevetted colonel in 1865 for "faithful and meritorious service," and in 1894 was awarded the Medal of Honor for bravery in action against the

Special Cases

Chiricahua Apaches.) "All the evidence in the case goes to show that he became intoxicated with the soldiers who subsequently assaulted him. They were all drinking and he got into a political argument with them which resulted in his being beat by them. I had the men confined in prison and he placed nominally in arrest and laid the matter before Major Genl. Hurlbut com'g the 16th Army Corps who thought it best to submit the matter to the Surgeon General, for his action in the matter." The Assistant Surgeon General, at St. Louis (whose signature is illegible) replied on May 24 and "…directs that you at once proceed to annul the contract of this officer." Richards was out, but not for long. One month later he was drawing a salary with Stoke's Battery of Horse Artillery, Cavalry Corps, 2nd Division, Army of the Cumberland. From then until March 1864, he was paid at two different sites: Beaufort, South Carolina, and Davenport, Iowa. It appears he was operating without a contract, and the surgeon general's office in Washington began looking into the matter, in a letter signed January 5, 1864, by Dr. Charles H. Crane, later brevetted brigadier general for "faithful and meritorious service." A letter, not in the file, from a surgeon of the 4th Ohio, settled this matter.

Richards seems to have applied for re-instatement. On June 1, 1864 a medical board, sitting at St. Louis, Missouri, found him qualified for the rank of Acting Assistant Surgeon, USA, and he was issued a fresh contract that same day. He managed to stay out of trouble for six months. On Feb. 4, 1865, John E. McGirr, surgeon at US General Hospital, Nashville, Tennessee, submitted a report. (McGirr was brevetted later that year for "faithful and meritorious service.")

In his report he noted that Richards had been relieved of duty "…for the reason that he is in the habit daily of prescribing more whiskey than is needed for the patients in his ward and when the bottles are returned filled from the Dispensary to the wards he abstracts from them & pours into bottles which he carries about his person. The amount of whiskey he has thus prescribed to excess (generally 12 ounces & sometimes 16 ounces daily) to drink it himself." In addition, Richards was writing prescriptions for medicines never used in that hospital, presumably for sale outside the hospital. The story was confirmed by Richards's confession and by the testimony of two other surgeons. On February 7, 1865, after a flurry of activity, noted in badly faded records, Richard had his contract annulled, and his papers marked "Black List." He was out again. And certainly there was no finding of "faithful and meritorious service." But his story isn't over yet.

The next entries in his records are dated 1891. A hasty scrawl reads, "The within was written by our Natick [Massachusetts] "Oracle" … and is the best I do for you. W. Richards." This followed by a clear rubber-stamped "Wm. Richards, M.D., Natick, Mass." In an entirely different hand, we see: "Natick April 21/91. Dr. Wm. Richards. Sir. I met Eliot Perry Esq. of South Natick yesterday. He is a cousin of the Richards I referred to in my note. "Wm." Richards went to New York in the early part of the War. Was in a dry goods house. After a few years he failed to communicate with his mother. The next heard of him was the report that he was captured and killed by the Indians in Arizona. Soon after a companion who escaped came to South Natick and related the circumstances of his death Mrs. Richards. The event occurred according to Mr. Perry's recollection some 15 years ago." The signature is hard to read.

Was Dr. Richards long dead in the Arizona desert, or practicing medicine in his hometown? Or is this even the same Dr. Richards? The 1890 census is not available. The 1900 census shows a physician William Richards, age 74, native of New York. He has been married to Martha for 38 years. Most likely this is not our Dr. Richards. We can be pretty sure that he was a drunk and a thief, but his life after 1865 remains a mystery. BL.

Frederick Swingley enlisted in the 59th Ohio Infantry June 22, 1862. He never actually served with the regiment, but was at the Huntsville, Alabama, Convalescent Barracks in July, at Camp Tod, Ohio, in September, and October and November at General Hospital No. 14 at Nashville. He resigned November 26, 1862. His reasons for serving only five months are unknown. On Christmas Eve 1862 he became a contract physician, signing up at Louisville, Kentucky. He gave his home as Bucyrus, Ohio.

He worked at Russellville, Kentucky, through February 1863, then at Louisville in March and April, and then was transferred to Camp Chase, Ohio, where he was stationed through March 1864. He began at Camp Chase treating newly drafted men (certainly many communicable diseases there) and then was moved to caring for prisoners. On the 14th of March, he was abruptly relieved of duty. On the 18th, Col. W. P. Richardson, 25th Ohio, commanding Camp Chase, wrote, "I have

Special Cases

relieved Dr. Swingley from attendance on the [Confederate] prisoners of war at this post … unsafe to permit him to have access to the prisoners." Swingley's offense? "Misconduct in furnishing liquor to Prisoners of War." His contract was terminated March 21, 1864.

Swingley traveled to Washington, DC, and acquired a new contract on May 23, 1864, apparently failing to mention his recent annulment at Camp Chase. He was put to work at a hospital in Alexandria, Virginia, where ten days later his past caught up with him. This contract, too, was terminated. He returned to Bucyrus where, on June 10th, he wrote a long letter to Joseph K. Barnes, Surgeon General of the US Army. He began with noting a one-day error in dating his contract, then launched into litany of complaints about the medical service, and ended by requesting a full investigation, including the testimony of the prisoners at Camp Chase. His plea availed him naught. Twenty-two years later, there was a final entry in his record. In 1886, he applied for a pension, asserting service-connected disability. The pension examiner reviewed his entire service record and concluded that there was not a single entry that might suggest disease or injury. Here his military records end. BL.

But there always more to every human story. In 1860, Swingley was age 50, living in Bucyrus with 40-year old Mary and their five children, ranging in age from 18 to nine. He was 52 when he enlisted, and maybe he was annoyed by all the young whipper-snappers around him. Maybe he figured the lonely, depressed Confederate prisoners needed a little nip of whiskey. Or maybe he faced hard times at home and needed his army pay. His June 30, 1900 obituary noted his age as 92, and that he had begun his practice in Bucyrus in 1834. His medical life spanned the introduction of both anesthesia and the concept of bacteria.

The Civil War proved longer, harder, and more widespread than anyone had predicted in 1861. Among the surprises was the vast number of prisoners, on both sides, who needed to be secured, housed, fed and kept reasonably healthy. One of the prison camps established by the Union was at Rock Island, Illinois. The island itself was in the Mississippi River, just opposite Davenport, Iowa. In 1860, it had been a sylvan paradise, but it was soon the scene of a vast prison, with dozens of barrack-like huts. Along with hundreds of guards, cooks, warehouseman, and laborers, there were doctors. Including Peter Arthur Baldwin, who was age 31 in 1863, living with his wife Helen, five years his junior, at Annawan, some forty miles east of Rock Island.

When the Civil War began, the Regular Army was scattered at small posts across the far west. As soon as the soldiers were called east, the Indians increased their resistance to white encroachment. One solution was "galvanizing." In its usual usage, this is plating a small layer of zinc onto a steel object. In 1863, it came to mean putting a Confederate prisoner of war into a Union uniform, making him a "Galvanized Yankee." Thousands of prisoners were offered the chance to exchange the miseries of prison life with the less austere miseries of fighting Indians in Kansas, Nebraska, and Colorado, in units designated as United States Volunteers. The 2nd and 3rd US Volunteers were recruited at Rock Island, and Dr. Baldwin, who signed his contract on Christmas Day 1863, was assigned to provide medical care to "men enlisted from the Rebel prisoners at this Prison for the frontier service of the United States."

Dr. Baldwin managed to work eleven months before getting in trouble. He had a pass allowing him access to the prison compound during working hours, and at night for emergencies. His access was for one purpose only – providing medical care. On November 26, 1864, 1st Lieut. Luther F. Wyman, assistant provost marshal of prisoners, filed a report, accusing Baldwin of entering the prison as much as six times a day, often for the purpose of trading in watches and clothing and bringing in, for sale, "whiskey or other intoxicating drinks." Further, while Medical Officer of the Day, Baldwin was not at his post in the prison, available for emergencies, but had crossed the Mississippi River to visit Davenport, Iowa.

A flurry of investigations by Wyman's superiors confirmed the accusations. A November 29 memo recommended that Baldwin's contract be terminated. On November 30, 1864, Dr. Baldwin addressed a brief note to Surgeon Charles S. Tripler, whose name is memorialized in the "Pink Palace," the famous Army hospital on the slopes above Honolulu. "I desire to have my contract annulled or suspended dating from November 29th. My business obliges me to go South at once." Here, Baldwin disappears from the military records. Did he develop Southern sympathies in seeing prison conditions? Or was he already sympathetic to the Confederacy? Or was he merely abusing his position to make a quick buck? And what urgent business called him South? He and his

Special Cases

wife were both born in New York State, suggesting no Southern roots and he was still at Annawan in 1870 and 1880. He left us more questions than answers. BL.

An old *New Yorker* cartoon shows a tombstone with the inscription, "I told you I was sick." Could this apply to the story of Wesley Blaisdell (Blaisdal) who, at the age of 45, was mustered into the 113th New York Infantry and resigned on October 1, 1862, after only two months of service? On November 13, 1862, just five weeks later, he enlisted in the 75th New York. (Shortly after he left the 113th New York Infantry it became the 7th New York Heavy Artillery.)

Four months later, he was stationed at Brashear City (now Morgan City) Louisiana. There, on March 15, 1863, he wrote a letter to the Surgeon General of the army. "I presume to address you because I have from personal observation and universal report been assured that you always reward merit yet I am compelled to bear testimony of myself." He added a piece of his history: When he was with the 113th New York, they were stationed at Newport News, Virginia, where he was "compelled to resign for obvious reasons." [He didn't specify these "obvious reasons."] Now he was with the 75th New York and, under orders from Gen. Godfrey Weitzel, was also providing medical care to the 6th Massachusetts, the 1st Maine Battery, the 1st Louisiana Regular Battery, and "Capt. Barratt's & Lieut. Perkins' two cavalry companies." He told his correspondent that he was treating the equivalent of a brigade, in a place full of sickness, and had not lost a patient. "I should be in justice receive a Surgeon's Appointment." To his letter he attached a list of twelve officers who could attest to his good work. It's not clear if he received his promotion, but on the Fourth of July, four months after his letter, he was discharged from the 75th New York, after seven month's service.

The following year, on May 20, 1864, apparently under contract, he was ordered to travel from New York to Washington. There he was ordered to Fairfax Seminary Hospital in Virginia. After a month in Fairfax, he requested a transfer. "I most respectfully ask if not incompatible with the public service that I be transferred to one of the U.S.A. Hospitals in the State of New York. My reason for the request is that since I have been to duty here I have suffered continually with Bilious Diarrhea and unless I am removed to a more Northern Climate respectfully ask that my contract be annulled." His superior, Surgeon Daniel P. Smith, wrote, "This officer can be spared." Blaisdell was out. Again. In July he wrote, enquiring about his pay for his month at Fairfax.

He was out, but not for long. On October 1, 1864 he signed a new contract assigning him to "Arkansas or elsewhere." Elsewhere turned out to be New Bern, North Carolina. He was posted to the General Hospital. After eight days at New Bern, he wrote again, listing four reasons he should relieved from "hospital practice." His reasons: "1st Physically of a bilious habit and temperament, 2nd Predisposition to Hepatic Disease, 3rd am now laboring under Engorgement of the liver, and require an active bilious cathartic, which I propose to take this day, 4th Twenty years Experience as a Physician with Army & Southern practice, as well as Northern, have learned some what to know myself." The medical director at New Bern, Daniel W. Hand, replied within hours. "Your contract … is terminated." Hand wrote to the Surgeon General that same day, stating that Blaisdell was terminated for "gross cowardice … the presence of Yellow Fever seemed to frighten him out of all propriety … we are grossly overworked, with two doctors down sick, but I have no use for such a man."

Dr. Hand was certainly no coward. He was brevetted colonel for "skill, energy, and fidelity during a severe Yellow Fever epidemic in the Autumn of 1864 at New Bern."

Sadly for patients and doctors, in 1864 the cause, prevention, and treatment of Yellow Fever were unknown. The cause is a mosquito-borne virus. Prevention is a combination of vaccine and anti-mosquito measures. Even today, there is no treatment, other than supportive measures. Dr. Hand battled Yellow Fever with two weapons: courage and the tendency for most patients to recover.

At this low point in his military career, let us consider why Blaisdell joined the army. Some of our misbehaving doctors seemed to need the money, but the 1860 census shows Blaisdell as a widower, with $40,000 in real estate and $31,000 in personal estate, a very wealthy man. His father, Levi, fought in the American Revolution. Maybe Wesley was simply patriotic.

And what of Dr. Blaisdell after his brief sojourn in fever-ridden North Carolina? He died at Grand Bridge Mills, Virginia, headed for his home

Special Cases

in New York, eight days after being terminated at New Bern. "I told you I was sick." BL.

In the old army, there was no retirement. One just held on to one's position until death intervened. Lincoln inherited Thomas Lawson, who had become surgeon general under John Quincy Adams. Lawson was a narrow, fastidious, senile penny-pincher with no sense of the huge armies now coming into being, but he could not be replaced, because he was still alive. When he fell into a coma, he could not be replaced, because he was still alive. Only when he was, in actual fact, dead, on May 15, 1861, could he be replaced. As Lawson drifted in and out of consciousness, this letter was addressed to him from 37-year old William B. Crouse, writing from Selinsgrove, Pennsylvania: "April 23, 1861. Dear Sir, Would there be any opportunity for being taken as Surgeon or Assistant. I would make very effort in my power to render myself useful in the Army. I love our glorious country and would do anything to save the Union. Would be willing to go as soon as I get the word. Hope I may soon hear from you. PS I am a graduate of Jefferson Medical College." The surgeon general's staff marked the letter, "Received April 27, 1861." This seemed like an auspicious beginning for a military career.

For possible personal reasons, there was no further action for twenty-two months, when on February 14, 1863, he signed a contract with the usual terms and stipulations, sending him to "Nashville or elsewhere." In 1860, Crouse was a graduate of the country's most prestigious medical school and living in Philadelphia with his wife, 25-year old Rebecca, and their two children. Yet he owned no real estate and only $300 of personal goods. Later in 1860, he moved his family 153 miles to Selinsgrove, Pennsylvania, a tiny hamlet of no consequence, certainly a step downward in the economic ladder. His desire to join the army may have been borne of desperation. So, off he went to Nashville.

There he was assigned to US General Hospital No. 19. After six months, he was suddenly transferred to Hospital No. 8. Just seven days later, Dr. Thomas Karber, in charge at No. 8, asked that Crouse be assigned elsewhere because of "frequent intoxication and professional incompetence." After being ejected from the army in mid-October, he was back on the staff of his alma mater. There, less than a month after his disgraceful departure from Nashville, he prevailed upon a medical school colleague (name illegible) to recommend him for re-appointment. "He informs me that all his relations with the medical officers and the [military] service were agreeable to him; and that he believes his own course was satisfactory." In November, two more doctors wrote glowing letters of recommendation. Especially touching was that of David Hayes Agnew who informed the surgeon general that Crouse had come home from Nashville because of a "super abundance" of doctors there.

Based on these documents, Crouse was re-appointed and put in charge of the Convalescent Hospital at St. Augustine, Florida, where he was in trouble again within sixty days. He had submitted a provision request with a false signature. "It was signed by the Hospital Steward, A. Racho, in accordance with my orders, I being so unwell that I could not at the time write my own name." His superiors suspected he was too drunk to write his own name, put him under arrest, and scheduled him for a court-martial, being charged with being so drunk that he could not perform his duty. However, as a civilian doctor he could not be court-martialed. On February 19, 1864 his contract was annulled for drunkenness. Crouse was finished. Or was he?

Sometime in the Spring of 1864 he obtained a commission as Assistant Surgeon, 38th US Colored Infantry, but was dismissed September 21, 1864.

In early October 1864 (the document is badly faded), he was issued yet another contract, and was assigned to Camp William Penn, near Philadelphia. Now, the surgeon general's staff was more alert. "Respectfully returned <u>Disapproved.</u> Dr. Crouse's former contract was annulled by the Medical Director, Dept. of the South, for drunkenness & inefficiency. Oct. 5, 1864."

On October 22, 1864, Dr. Crouse wrote a most remarkable letter, addressed to "Medical Director," in which he claimed that his Nashville service had been "one year or more." At St. Augustine, he was the victim of "false charges." Since then, "I served six months in Commission (38th USCT?) and honorably mustered out of the service at my own request. For references as to my character I can give the best Philadelphia can produce." Is this the product of alcoholic blackouts, Wernicke-Korsakoff Syndrome, or simply a pack of lies? (The syndrome, common in advanced alcoholism, includes inventing stories to cover memory gaps.) That same day, October 22, Crouse had scheduled himself for an

Special Cases

examination for a fresh commission in the US Colored Troops. Because of his record, that examination was never held.

And what of Crouse after the war? By 1870 he had moved his family from obscure Selinsgrove, Pennsylvania to the even more remote hamlet of Posey, tucked into the southwest corner of Indiana. There he is listed as "physician," with no assets, while his wife Rebecca owned $1500 in real estate. Their 16-year old son James was working as a farm laborer. A decade later, he is "retired, at age 54, because of general debility." His grown sons are still at home, working as clerks.

Pensions were usually reserved for those soldiers who had served honorably, yet both Crouse and his wife received pensions. How did Crouse get a pension? In 1886, he filed for an invalid pension, based on his brief service with the 38th US Colored Troops. At his 1886 medical examination he was 5-feet, 5-inches tall and weighed 98 pounds. His diagnoses: "Chronic diarrhea and disease of the kidneys." On April 23, 1886, his application was rejected because of being "dishonorably discharged." He immediately embarked on collecting records, not only those from his 1864 service, but many sworn affidavits from survivors of his brigade. These voluminous and often contradictory records may be summarized as follows.

Crouse's chief antagonist seems to have been Col. Alonzo G. Draper, 36th US Colored Troops. (Draper was brevetted brigadier general in 1864 and died of an "accidental gunshot wound" in 1865.) Draper left several statements describing Crouse as "beastly drunk." A four-page 1886 affidavit by John T. Strong, formerly surgeon of the 44th US Colored Troops, paints a different story. Paraphrased: "I never saw any sign of intoxication. The only person who claimed Crouse was drunk was Col. Draper, who swore that if Crouse got any discharge it would be a dishonorable one. I witnessed a very heated discussion between Col. Draper and Surgeon Hall Davis, 38 US Colored Troops. Davis said that Crouse's condition was from diarrhea, heat exhaustion, and malaria; Draper said Crouse's only problem was alcohol. Davis replied, "Let Crouse resign before he dies." Strong was very concerned about Draper's "vicious and malicious spirit."

In Crouse's own affidavit he claimed to have contracted diarrhea and Bright's disease while at Deep Bottom, Virginia, and over the succeeding years had sought a restorative climate at Spring Hollow and Butler in Missouri, at Cloverland and Brazil in Indiana, and at Summit in

Illinois. Two affidavits, both done in September 1864, certify the Crouse had discharged his duties "faithfully, promptly, and skillfully." They were provided by Surgeons Hall Davis, 38th US Colored Troops, and Arthur H. Cowdrey, 37th US Colored Troops.

Other documents state that Crouse was dismissed for drunkenness and neglect. Draper wrote that "[Crouse] acknowledges that he was guilty of cowardice in the presence of his regiment on [August 5, 1864] at the time of the explosion of the rebel mine." Draper claimed that the Davis had said – in a sort of double hearsay – that Dr. Alfred A. Woodhull, on meeting Crouse, had said, "I could not tell if he was drunk or crazy." (Woodhull retired in 1900 as Assistant Surgeon General of the US Army.)

Lt. Col. Abial G. Chamberlain, 37th US Colored Troops did not support Crouse's claims. He had twice found Crouse "beastly drunk" and twice had kept him after Crouse "took the pledge."

Where ever truth lies in all of this, we do know that in 1888 Congressional Special Bill No. 762, 50th Congress, 1st Session, changed Crouse's discharge to "honorable," opening the way to a pension. On his death in 1892, his widow began receiving her pension. BL. UW.

John R. McCullough entered the Federal records on November 25, 1863 at Albany, New York, when he was appointed an assistant surgeon with the 82nd New York Infantry. He was forty-four. Within a month he was court-martialed for being too drunk to attend to a dying lieutenant and for being boisterously drunk on New Years Eve, at Stevensburg, Virginia. He was cashiered (dishonorably discharged).

He apparently obtained a contract, because he appears as acting assistant surgeon on the steamboat *City Point* in early September 1864, being arrested for selling liquor to enlisted men, at fifty cents to $1.00 a shot. (Roughly two day's wages for a private.) A week later, he was ordered to board a ship bound for the Department of the Gulf, but missed the boat and went elsewhere, apparently back to Albany, New York. In late September, for the liquor sales, for borrowing and not returning money from soldiers and from the laundress, and for not following orders, his contact was annulled. (His pay records for 28 days in September 1864 showed him at McDougall General Hospital in New York Harbor, on board the *City Point*, and at the US General Hospital at Albany, New York). He was out of the army. Again.

Special Cases

Three months later he was back, this time at Milwaukee, Wisconsin, where he signed a new contract, to work at "Nashville, or elsewhere, or on Hospital Trains." On May 1, 1865 he was at Chicago, where he wrote requesting a commission. This letter contains at least two bold-faced lies, shameless fabrications. He accounted for leaving the 82nd New York by claiming that they were being mustered out, when in fact the regiment was in service until June 1864. He left, as we have seen earlier, because he was charged, tried, convicted, and ejected by a general court-martial. He also claimed that his prior contract had been annulled at his request in order to attend to family business in New York, when the real cause was that he was cheating soldiers – and even the poor laundress – as well as selling whiskey illegally. A nearly illegible reply, on May 16, 1865 informed McCullough that while he seemed professionally qualified there was no need for more surgeons. (At this point, the war was over.) In July 1865, he served briefly with the 1st Ohio Sharpshooters. On July 22 he was assigned to be assistant surgeon with the 110th US Colored Troops, however "… after a careful examination both written and oral on Medical, Surgical & the collateral sciences, he was found not qualified to be an assistant surgeon of colored troops." From this point, he worked briefly at two more places: Chattanooga, August through November 1865, and Nashville Smallpox Hospital, December 14, 1865 to February 18, 1866, when he requested annulment of his 1865 contract. In 1886 his request for a pension was rejected.

Who was McCullough as a person? In the census records for 1850 through 1880 there are seventy-five John McCulloughs. Only one was a physician and his age and location are wrong. He was most likely Irish, but beyond that he remains a mystery as a person and a failure as a doctor. BL. (LL1368).

In the summer of 1864, a 25-year old Canadian physician, Charles Petit Pitcher, crossed the border and on June 10, 1864, at Detroit, Michigan, signed a contract. Five days later, he reported for duty at Jefferson General Hospital, at Jeffersonville, Indiana. An unrecorded transfer sent him to Asylum General Hospital, at Knoxville, Tennessee. There on July 6, 1864, he was Officer of the Day, the only surgeon on duty.

Pitcher drank a substantial quantity of hospital whiskey, went into several wards where he "performed delicate operations," cursed the ladies in the Extra Diet Kitchen, waved a loaded pistol at the hospital clerk, went into the street, and, brandishing his naked sword blade above his head, marched into town. The next day, he was sent to the provost marshal, "for transmission out of the Department of the Ohio." His contract was annulled for "beastly drunkenness and … total unreliability." Back home, his bride, Clara, whom he had married the year before, when she was seventeen, awaited his return. The Ontario census of 1881 shows them still together. In the 1891 census she is a widow.

On October 22, 1882, she filed a pension application based on his American military service. There are several notes trying to locate him, including one from Dr. Sheldon Pitcher of Detroit, apparently not a close relative, who responded, "Dr. Chas. P. Pitcher left home in 1864 and [I] have not had tidings from him since. Would like to know myself where he is." Clara never completed the application process. Charles may have set some sort of record, being discharged in disgrace after less than a month of service. BL.

William G. Scott was commissioned as a surgeon in the 8th Indiana Cavalry on April 7, 1863. He resigned May 15, 1863, after just five weeks of service. His regiment had one action near Scott's time of duty, but it was a skirmish at Middleton, Tennessee, a week after he resigned. (While he was with the regiment, it was re-designated the 8th Mounted Infantry.) We meet him next in Nashville, Tennessee, less than three months later, when he was tried and convicted by a military commission. Scott was then a contract surgeon, in charge of Hospital No. 5. He stole $100 worth of coffee from the hospital stores, a value of at least $3,000 in today's money. He put the coffee in the hands of a Mrs. Manning, a prostitute with whom he was living. A short time later, they sold the coffee to one Mollie May, a prostitute living on Jefferson Street. A sutler who had visited the Scott-Manning love nest testified that he had seen "crushed sugar and coffee there," and knew that the two slept in the same bed. Before the verdict, it was customary for the defendant to submit a written defense, which Scott did. It is such a masterpiece of breath-taking irrelevance, Victorian efflorescence, and inflated verbosity that it merits reproduction in its entirety, and appears as Appendix C.

Special Cases

In spite of his verbal Arabesques the court convicted him and sentenced Scott to repay the government $100 and stay in prison until it was paid, after which, "He be sent out of this Department, and not permitted to return during the war .. a copy of this to be sent to the Surgeon General." Are we done with Scott? Not yet.

He applied for a pension in 1892, listing as his wife one Mary Roberts. The pension examiner asked for proof of marriage. (The National Archives pension files are full of original wedding licenses.) Scott replied that the presiding minister had failed to file the proper papers. Then, he was asked to prove his own date of birth. Scott submitted a Bible with an 1839 birth date written in it. The pension examiner noted that the Bible was printed in 1856! In 1911, Scott filed a claim for clothing he had lost during the Civil War. As a final note, he claimed service in the 8th Indiana Mounted Infantry, in which he served only five weeks. In the end, Scott got nothing. (NN697).

Samuel H. Anderson, Asst. Surgeon, 4th Kentucky Cavalry (Confederate) seemed more interested in killing people than in healing them. Confederate General John Hunt Morgan's "Great Raid" in the summer of 1863 included a scouting expedition into southern Indiana, commanded by Capt. Henry Hines, 9th Kentucky Cavalry. Hines' eighty-man company, dressed in Federal uniforms (a good way to get hanged as a spy), was quickly detected and was pursued night and day by Federal cavalry and Union home guards. Days in the saddle without sleep soon had the skin sloughing off the men's legs and the horses stumbling with fatigue. Staggering back to the north bank of the Ohio River, most of the men surrendered. Hines swam the river and escaped into Confederate territory. Among those captured was a 32-year old man with black hair, dark eyes, and dark complexion, five feet, nine inches tall. This was our Dr. Anderson.

Anderson first appears in the Union records in a memo dated July 3, 1863, sent by Brig. Gen. Jeremiah T. Boyle to Col. "Mark Mundy" (probably Marcellus Mundy, 23rd Kentucky Infantry [Union]) commanding the post at Louisville. "You will send to the commanding officer, Cincinnati, Ohio, under charge of a trusty non-comd. Officer, Samuel Anderson, Asst. Surgn., 4th Rebel Kentucky Cavly. captured at Leavenworth, Indiana June 12th in company with Hine's band of guerrillas, to be forwarded into Confederate lines. You will send with him a statement of the facts of his capture."[1]

Anderson was "forwarded" in a very circuitous manner. In late July, he was at Camp Chase, near Columbus, Ohio. In August, listed as "exchanged," he was sent to Old Capitol Prison in Washington, DC. Two months later he was in prison at Fort McHenry, in Baltimore's inner harbor. From there, he was sent to City Point, Virginia, and passed into Confederate lines. December 1863 found him suffering from diarrhea, under treatment at Floyd House and Ocmulgee Hospital, at Macon, Georgia. He seemed to have recuperated quickly and by Spring 1864 was robbing and murdering in southern Missouri.

Ten months passed before he next appeared in the Union records, ten months in which he was very active. The paraphrased records of the provost marshal at Rolla, Missouri, tell the story. May 2, 1864. From Reed to J. P. Sanderson at St. Louis. Re: affidavits against S. H. Anderson. Anderson was connected with a band of robbers and murderers, his associate [Thomas] One-Armed Brown is probably the murderer of Fowlkes. Brown and Bill Wilson, another of the crowd, were two of the worst guerrillas in Missouri. No one will swear that Anderson was present when Fowlkes was killed and Fields wounded, but the evidence is clear Brown and Wilson were both present. Fowlkes and Brown were both quiet, loyal, and exemplary citizens. Fowlkes was more than 60 years old. Anderson should be tried by a military commission. Of his guilt, there is no doubt.[2]

Reed wrote to Sanderson again on August 15, 1864. Paraphrased, Reed's message was: Guerrilla S. H. Anderson confined at Fort Wyman [Rolla] is sick and will die if not removed from the fort. But Rolla hospital is not secure and he will probably escape if placed there. I ask permission to send Anderson to St. Louis. Seven days later the commanding officer at Fort Wyman was ordered to bring Anderson to the provost marshal's office in an ambulance, so that he could be sent to St. Louis. That same day, Reed wrote to Sanderson again, relaying that when Anderson had learned of his death sentence it "roused" him. "He is clear of fever, still very feeble, and wants to go to St. Louis." On August 24th, Reed wrote to the prisoner, apparently in response to a letter from Anderson. Reed asked him to provide information. Which men were in the guerrilla scouting party? Who had ordered the scout? What were the events that ended in Fowlkes' death and Fields' wounding? (We found no record

Special Cases

of Anderson answering such questions.) Meanwhile, Anderson had been writing frequent letters to President Lincoln, and Reed had sent a full report, regarding Anderson, to the provost marshal general in St. Louis.

On September 22, 1864, Brig. Gen. John McNeil wrote to Maj. Gen. William Rosecrans that Anderson's sentence of death by hanging had been suspended "until further order." McNeil described Anderson as a leader, not a follower, in guerrilla warfare, and a doctor of high social standing. McNeil thought it unfair that Joseph Johnson, convicted with Anderson, should die, while Anderson should be reprieved. Johnson was an "ignorant dolt," while Anderson was highly educated. McNeil thought Anderson's death would be a better example to the public. Johnson was hanged December 21, 1864, and his corpse dropped into an unmarked grave.[3]

Anderson's trial by military commission, held in June 1864, convicted him of belonging to the guerrilla band of One-Armed Brown. In company with William Wilson and one Copeland, they pillaged and plundered the loyal citizens of Phelps County, Missouri. In addition, Anderson was active in "Sonner's" [Sommer's?] band of bushwhackers, and had made threats to kill every loyal Union man he could find. Anderson was sentenced to hang, a decision endorsed by Rosecrans, who then sent the case to Lincoln for approval. Lincoln's Judge Advocate General, Joseph Holt, returned the case to Rosecrans, advising him that he had full power to execute Anderson, and did not need presidential approval. In the president's own hand, we see: "View of Judge Advocate General approved. A. Lincoln Sep.6, 1864."[4]

Meanwhile, Anderson, from his jail cell, had sent out a flood of letters, poems, and prayers, most of them addressed to Lincoln, but he did not ignore Grenville Dodge, who also received a flood of literary creations. Dodge, now a major general and commanding the Department of Missouri (and future genius of the Union Pacific Railway) seemed swayed by Anderson's efforts. He wrote to Lincoln, recommending that Anderson's death sentence be commuted to a prison term. Lincoln, like the proverbial man who failed at throwing away his boomerang, once again had Anderson on his desk. Lincoln's secretary, John Hay, wrote: "The recommendation of Gen. Dodge is approved. Let the prisoner be

Bad Doctors

confined at hard labor during the war. Feb 9, 1865." Lincoln signed the order. Anderson had escaped the noose, but not controversy.

In May 1875, the case of *State of Missouri vs. S.H. Anderson* was tried in Oregon County. The first degree manslaughter charge noted that "…on the 1st day of April 1874 upon the body of Louisa Seats … then and there pregnant with a quick child willfully, unlawfully and feloniously and with intent to destroy such child did use and employ an instrument, to wit, a pair of scissors, and with said scissors did crush the skull of said child … the destroying of said child not being necessary to preserve the life of the mother." For reasons related to complex local politics, the prosecutor "entered a Nolle prosequi." Anderson was off the hook – again. Mrs. Seats' motivation in all this may be explained by her May 1875 divorce from William R. Seats, who seems to have been a violent, brawling drunk. The 1880 census shows Anderson still in Oregon County. His wife Sarah and daughter Margaret were both born in Illinois. The Missouri Medical Society has no record of him. Here he fades from history. (Prepared with the considerable help of John Bradbury, Lou Wehmer, and Beverly A. Lowry.)

NOTES
1. Leavenworth is on the north bank of the Ohio River.
2. National Archives Record Group 393 (RG393) pt. 4, e1764, Records of subordinate provost marshals, Dept. of the Missouri, Vols. 666-669, 742. Vol. 666/1637.
3. RG393, pt. 2, e3323 – Letters sent. (Nos. 295-689 & 296/691 DMo) District of Rolla.
4. RG153, Records of the Judge Advocate General's Office (Army) e15, court-martial case file NN2144.

Chapter Three

United States Navy Surgeons

The Civil War Union navy was far smaller than the Union army. The army totaled 2,677,097 soldiers and officers, while the navy totaled 101,207 sailors and officers. There were 75,964 general courts-martial in the army and 1,441 general courts-martial in the navy. The army generated general courts-martial at twice the rate as the navy: 2.8 percent, compared with 1.4 percent. Nine navy surgeons were court-martialed. The navy trials are numbered differently from those of the army: numerals alone with no letters. All the navy's courts-martial are on microfilm M273, 198 rolls of 35 mm. film, cited as Records of General Courts-Martial & Courts of Inquiry of the Navy Department, 1799-1867. The navy courts-martial were read and indexed by Beverly A. Lowry in 2000-2001.

Babin, Hosea.
> Surgeon. USS *Stonewall*. He allowed the ship to become unsanitary on the voyage from Havana, Cuba to Washington, DC. A father testified that Babin failed to diagnose yellow fever in his son, allowing the boy to die. Babin was dismissed. (4357). However, he must have been re-instated, since records show him as a Navy surgeon from February 10, 1865 to December 15, 1904.

Duvall, Marius.
> Surgeon. USS *New Ironsides*. He made false charges against other officers, including claiming that a lieutenant commander had spoken ill of Admiral Dahlgren. A court of inquiry recommended

court-martial. (4306). The court-martial itself occupied many hundreds of pages, and included charges that he gave whiskey to the crew of the captain's gig of the USS *Winona*, that he improperly endorsed a Marine's sick ticket, that he made many false and insubordinate statements, etc., etc. He was sentenced to be suspended from duty for six months, and be reprimanded by the Secretary of the Navy. (3606).

Gibson, (first name not recorded).

Surgeon. USS *New Hampshire*. On board the ship, he inflicted an illegal punishment. A court of inquiry says he did so. (4614).

Johnson, William.

Surgeon. Norfolk, Virginia Naval Hospital. He was drunk and failed to investigate the management of the hospital. Accused of red eyes. Defense witness said, "Prisoner has an affliction of the tarsal glands and a slight pterygium, which causes a congestion of the conjunctiva." Acquitted. (4313).

Kershner, Edward.

Asst. Surgeon. USS *New Ironsides*. Wrote an article about the attack on the forts in Charleston's harbor, which reflected on Rear Admiral DuPont, sent the article to the Baltimore *American*, which published it. Kershner was dismissed. (3253).

Sharp, Solomon.

Surgeon. Norfolk, Virginia Naval Hospital. He was accused of being drunk, but "prisoner is afflicted with partial paralysis by which his speech is impaired." Also accused of mismanagement. Acquitted. He was tried with William Johnson. (4313).

Suddards, James.

Surgeon. Naval Asylum at Philadelphia. Orders were posted forbidding leaving the grounds. He left anyway. Suddards told the court that he felt no need to obey the orders, "on principle." He was suspended for six months, without pay, and reprimanded by the Secretary of the Navy. (3603).

Woodward, Roland E.

Surgeon. USS *Commodore Perry*. He quarreled with Acting Ensign R. W. Elwell, at Gosport, Virginia. Elwell had called Woodward "a liar" and threatened to throw him overboard. Acquitted. (4393).

This small number suggests no generality, except the possibility that a deeper look at the career of the *New Ironsides* might be interesting. She generated twelve general courts-martial during her Civil War career and has twenty-five entries in the index of *Civil War Naval Chronology 1861-1865*, a three-inch thick reference book, published by the Department of the Navy in 1971.

Chapter Four
Confederate Surgeons

(See Appendix B)

Anderson, Samuel H.
> Asst. Surgeon. 4th Kentucky Cavalry. He traveled with a gang of Missouri bushwhackers, including One-Armed Brown, and was convicted of murder. His life contained much further turmoil. See Special Cases chapter.

Armstrong, James G.
> Asst. Surgeon. 17th North Carolina. Disobedience. Acquitted. (anv1279).

Baden, Joseph Abell.
> Asst. Surgeon. 4th Division, Camp Winder Hospital. He was tried for "Conduct unbecoming an officer and a gentleman," and acquitted. The legal officer involved was Capt. James H. Pearce, Asst. Adj. General, Wise's Brigade. Pearce himself was tried for drunkenness in June 1863 (G.O. #2) and acquitted because he was fatigued from a scout and no longer in the presence of the enemy.

Baptist, William H.
> Surgeon. 9th Alabama and 5th Florida. Court-martialed three times. Forty-second Article of War. Reprimanded. (anv0265). Again, 42nd Article of War (lying out of camp). Fined a month's pay. (mc g.o. 92). Conduct prejudicial. Fined two month's pay. (anv0988).

Brown, James F.
: Asst. Surgeon. 7th Georgia. Violated 7th Article of War, and habitually drunk. Dismissed. (anv0393).

Butler, Jasper F.
: Surgeon. 13th Arkansas. No details in file. (shsp, vol. 22).

Cowherd, Colby.
: Asst. Surgeon. 13th Virginia. AWOL. Reprimanded with loss of one month's pay. (anv0879).

Evans, C. L.
: Asst. Surgeon. Possibly in "Confederate Generals & Staff." suggests Mike Musick (now-retired senior archivist). Filed false returns at Camp Moore, Tangipahoa Parish, Louisiana. (CMSR).

Flake, J. J.
: Asst. Surgeon. 3rd Alabama Cavalry. Drunk and AWOL. Cashiered. Gen. Longstreet orders him put in the ranks as a conscript. (glc g.o. 23).

Flore, Frederick.
: Asst. surgeon. 1st Missouri State Guards. Court-martialed by Federal authorities. See roster.

Foulkes, James F.
: Surgeon. 52nd North Carolina. "Violated Paragraph 438" (This paragraph is an obsessive's nightmare, which uses twenty-one lines of print to say, "Don't go out of channels".) Reprimanded. (anv0986).

Gibson, D. R.
: Asst. Surgeon. St. Paul Battalion of Foot Rifles of Louisiana. Disobedience. Acquitted. (anv0216).

Gott, Lewis (Louis) E.
: Surgeon. 21st Georgia. AWOL. Reprimanded. Court lenient because "he tried to get on the train, but could not." (anv1329).

Hamilton, Alexander D.
: Surgeon. Provisional Army of the Confederate States. Drunk. Acquitted. (anv0868). An A. D. Hamilton of the 5th Alabama was tried for neglect of duty and acquitted. (anv0918).

Harris, J. O.
: Asst. Surgeon. Provisional Army of the Confederate States. Tried for conduct unbecoming an officer and a gentleman. Acquitted. (mc g.o. 18).

Harrison, B. C.
>Asst. Surgeon. 28th Virginia. AWOL ten days at Richmond, Virginia, and twenty-four hours at Petersburg, Virginia. Fined one month's pay. (mc 9 pg. 152).

Hay, William.
>Surgeon. Staunton Hospital. Kept a sergeant as a wardmaster for five months. Acquitted. Also served in the 33rd Virginia. (anv0791).

Holt, Pleasant A.
>Surgeon. 6th North Carolina (Pender's Brigade). AWOL. Fined ten day's pay. (anv0794).

I'anson, Richard Walter.
>Surgeon. 2nd North Carolina Cavalry. Neglect of duty. Acquitted. Life dates 1830-1888. (anv1177).

Meiere, William Stack.
>Surgeon. Phillips Legion, Georgia. A court of inquiry regarding his failure to visit the hospitalized men at Hardeeville, South Carolina. They found him culpable and recommended a court-martial. (mc meiere).

Merritt, Thomas D.
>Asst. Surgeon. 18th Mississippi. Drunk on duty, misbehavior before the enemy, and theft of hospital stores. The court could not agree on a judgment and forwarded the record to Gen. Longstreet, who dismissed the charges. (glc g.o. 22).

Montgomery, W. T.
>Surgeon. 55th North Carolina (formerly with the 5th Alabama). Conduct prejudicial to good order and military discipline. Acquitted. (anv0918).

Moore, J. P.
>Surgeon. 10th Tennessee. AWOL two weeks from a leave of absence over Christmas 1863. Pleaded guilty, but acquitted. (rg109, box 94 and mc g.o. 22).

O'Hagan, Charles J.
>Surgeon. 35th North Carolina. Incompetent. The Richmond *Examiner* reported him to be "ignorant, disabled or incompetent." 16th Mississippi. Acquitted. (anv0332).

Peete, Richard Samuel Fennell.
>Surgeon. 12th North Carolina. AWOL. Acquitted. (anv1065).

Bad Doctors

Silliman, James.
> Asst. Surgeon. Provisional Army of the Confederate States. Sold three pints of government whiskey at Tullahoma, Tennessee. Acquitted. (mc hardee 45).

Snell, A. B.
> Surgeon. 16th Mississippi. Drunk. Cashiered. Sentence approved by R. E. Lee. (anv0411).

Trice, T. S.
> Asst. Surgeon. 5th Florida. Acquitted of drunkenness and embezzlement. Convicted of conduct prejudicial. Dismissed. (anv0988).

Upshur, Thomas H.
> Asst. Surgeon. Provisional Army of the Confederate States. Drunk. Reprimanded and suspended from rank one month. (nara g.o. page 8 and mc P&W 2333).

Waring, James J.
> Surgeon. Provisional Army of the Confederate States. At Kinston, North Carolina, refused to turn over medical stores, and refused to be relieved of his duties. Outcome and findings unknown. (mc Anderson).

Chapter Five
Conclusions

We have been able to identify nearly 622 disciplinary actions against Union army physicians/surgeons during the Civil War. Was this a lot or a little? In what perspective can we place these events? How does this incidence of discipline compare with non-medical Civil War troops, and how does it compare with the rate of disciplinary actions against today's doctors?

We will base this discussion primarily upon Union records. The comparable records for Confederate doctors are lost, or scattered, or in disarray. Perhaps some future writers will find the time and patience to seek out those records and analyze them. Only then can Union medical misbehavior properly be compared with Confederate medical malfeasance.

The Union armies had roughly 2.7 million men and 75,960 general courts-martial, a rate of 2.8 per cent. The Union forces had approximately 12,000 doctors (both commissioned and contract) and approximately 600 were court-martialed and/or dismissed, a rate of 5.0 percent – almost twice the rate of non-medical forces.

This is a most remarkable finding, but does it mean anything? Statistics are subject to many "confounding variables" (a lovely term) and here are some of them. Enlisted men were subject to two types of courts-martial. Regimental courts-martial were for lesser offenses. General courts-martial were more serious offenses, and could condemn men to death. The regimental trial records are widely scattered, often missing, and are hard to study. The Union general courts-martial are neatly filed in one archive and form the basis for our court-martial database. Commissioned officers could not be tried by regimental trials; for them it was a general court-martial or no court-martial at all. (The exception is "direct dismissal," discussed at length in *Utterly Worthless*.) Thus, even if a doctor's offense was minor, his trial would be a general court-martial.

We must consider at least two other factors. The percent acquitted would suggest that some charges were trivial, ill-founded, or frivolous. More important, what crimes were <u>medical</u> crimes as opposed to more general offenses, such as absence without leave or insubordination?

Reviewing all 75,960 Union general courts-martial, seventeen percent ended in acquittal. The comparable figure for doctors was fourteen percent, a rather similar finding. As for alcohol involvement, we found it in 14,049 of the 75,960 courts-martial – eighteen percent. In the court-martial records which describe a Union doctor with alcohol difficulties, the comparable figure is sixteen percent – 97 out of 600.

However, these figures mean very little, because hundreds of our cases were men ejected from the army by "direct dismissal," with little or no detail given in the published records. True some were cited for "drunkenness," but other cases involving alcohol may be subsumed under such rubrics as "incompetence" or "uncourteous behavior." Being slightly tipsy was so common in the 1860s, it seems certain that what a blood alcohol test would reveal today would go unremarked during the Civil War.

Even with all these caveats, it does seem that our figures show drunkenness to be no more common among doctors than it was among privates or colonels. The stereotype of the "drunken sawbones" is more a product of Hollywood and bad novels than of objective reality.

As to actual medical malpractice, as exhibited in bad diagnoses, bad surgery, bad prescribing, and/or cruel and heartless treatment of patients, we found sixty-six cases, out of our 600 identified malfeasants. There were 12,000 Union surgeons. The sixty-six men indicate that 0.5 percent of all Union surgeons committed identifiable malpractice in the years 1861-1865, or roughly 0.12 percent per year. How does this compare with doctors today? A mainstream, mid-west state may give us an answer.

In 2009, there were 10,375 physicians with active State of Iowa licenses. In that same year, there was a total of thirty-three "formal

Conclusions

disciplinary actions." These included license surrender, license suspension, and physicians placed on probation. That same year 458 complaint files were opened and 183 physicians continued under "Disciplinary Monitoring." Using the figures for formal disciplinary actions, 0.32 percent of Iowa physicians were subject to such action in that one year. Using the 0.12 and 0.32 percentages, one could venture an opinion that Civil War doctors were better behaved than their present-day confreres, perhaps three times better behaved. Certainly this comparison may be an egregious case of comparing apples and oranges, and rest on a slender reed indeed, given the documentation of 150 years ago, but it does suggest that our Civil War surgeons were not such a bad lot after all.

The possible flaws in such a conclusion are many. Alcohol and malpractice are often conjoined twins. One author, in his forty years of medical practice, has held several positions that included monitoring problem doctors. It's hard to imagine a doctor with a drinking problem who isn't also on the road to some therapeutic misadventure, so the exact degree of patient harm during the Civil War will remain forever beyond our reach.

And what of the hundreds of doctors whose offenses lay elsewhere than drunkenness or malpractice? These cover an easy-to-imagine spectrum: absence without leave, insubordination, theft, and embezzlement. And a remarkable number involved food, the preparation, serving, and payment thereof. Clarifying this subject may best be illuminated by a brief essay into Jewish dietary laws and the rules of kosher. In addition to the well-known prohibition of pork, there are the rules regarding the mixing of meat (*Fleishik*) and dairy products (*Milchik*). They may not be cooked together, served together, or consumed together. A dish or bowl, once used for meat becomes *Fleishik* and may not used to serve dairy products. The same for a dish used to serve milk, butter, or cheese; it has become forever *Milchik* and may not be used for meat. A proper kosher household will have two separate China services. The same rules apply to cooking utensils. A pot used to cook meat may not be used to warm milk. So like dishes and bowls, a kosher kitchen will have pots and kettles devoted solely to one class of food or another. How is this relevant to our Civil War doctors?

Today if a doctor enters the armed services he or she receives instruction in military rules and etiquette. In 1861-1865, the Articles of War and the Rules and Regulations contained *nothing* which would guide a new doctor, in particular, the rules for food derived from European armies. In Germany or England, for example, the regimental headquarters and officers' mess would be a building hallowed by time and tradition, and decorated with captured flags, ancient swords, and commemorative silver tureens. The enlisted men had the barracks. Officers and men did not dine together. Ever. Officers were gentlemen. Enlisted men were of a lower class.

In the American army, at the small posts that dotted the country before 1861, the gulf between officers and men was easy to maintain. Part of this separation involved food. The enlisted men were fed by the army. The officers formed a "mess," bought their own cooking gear, pooled their money to buy groceries, and hired cooks and servants. Officers did not eat the soldier's food, and vice versa. An army in the field, an army drawn from the egalitarian American population, was different. Imagine a volunteer regiment, after marching for weeks, camped in a desolate forest. The doctor has set up a small hospital, maybe just a tent or two, for the sick and the wounded. He is assisted by a hospital steward and a few soldiers, detailed to be nurses. After a day tending the patients, they gather for supper. A fallen log is their dining room. By army regulation, the steward and the nurses eat regimental food, cooked in kettles that belong to the regiment, hence belonging to the Federal government. The doctor, *au contraire*, is supposed to buy local meat and produce, in an area picked clean by foragers, cook it in his own personal pot, and eat it with his own utensils, sitting nowhere near his staff. An obsessive's nightmare, yet many doctors were court-martialed for crimes such as "forming a mess with enlisted men," with convoluted testimony regarding which kettle held government food and which held personal food, and did the doctor buy his own potato? These court-martial transcripts, with their almost endless quest for details, will remind some readers of the most tortured Talmudic disquisitions.

The remainder of the trials, after eliminating drunkenness, medical malpractice, and food issues, cover the gamut: absence without leave, insubordination, theft, bribery, and quarrels over precedence. Of course the biology and technology of medical practice were different. Our Civil War doctor had never heard of bacteria, viruses, antiseptics, sterile techniques, x-rays, antibiotics, or lab tests. There were no courses

Conclusions

in military customs or etiquette. Yet by their standards – not ours – they did remarkably well.

To sum up, our doctors of the 1860s seem little different from their non-medical colleagues, and much the same as the doctors of today. The great majority did their work faithfully, obeyed the rules, and brought honor to their ancient profession. One cannot ask more than that.

Appendix A
Union Sources and Citations

(NN210). File Folder No. NN210, National Archives Record Group 153, Records of the Judge Advocate General's Office (Army), Entry 15, Court-martial case files. Army courts-martial files have two letters, followed by a number.

(2315). US Navy Court-martial No. 2315. M273, Records of General Courts-Martial & Courts of Inquiry of the Navy Department, 1799-1867. One hundred-ninety eight rolls of 35 mm. microfilm. Navy courts-martial are catalogued by numbers but no letters.

BL. "Black List." Formally National Archives Record Group 112, Surgeon General's Office, Entry 144, Contract Surgeons Considered Unfit for Re-employment – Black List.

Heitman. *Historical Register and Dictionary of the U.S. Army.* Vol. I. Author: Francis B. Heitman. Publisher: Government Printing Office, Washington, DC. Published 1903, republished by the University of Illinois Press at Urbana, 1965.

RRS. *A Roster of All the Regimental Surgeons and Assistant Surgeons in the Late War and Hospital Service.* Authors: Newton Allen Strait and J. E. Wells. Publisher: G. M. Van Buren, Washington, DC. Published 1883.

TS. *Tarnished Scalpels – The Courts-martial of Fifty Union Surgeons.* Authors: Thomas P. Lowry and Jack D. Welsh. Stackpole Books. Published 2000.

UW. *Utterly Worthless – One Thousand Delinquent Union Officers Deemed Unworthy of a Court-martial.* Author: Thomas P. Lowry. Booksurge. Published 2010.

Appendix B
Confederate Sources and Citations

Researching the records of Union military justice is relatively simple – all general courts-martial are in one huge file in the National Archives, neatly laid out in numbered folders and boxes. There are not one but two indices: the hand-written name index created in the 1800s and the computer-based one created by the Index Project in the decade 1995-2005 by Beverly A. and Thomas P. Lowry.

The Confederacy, on the other hand, burned all their court-martial transcripts when they set fire to their own capital in April 1865. Happily, the General Orders of the Army of Northern Virginia survived and have been microfilmed. (Sadly, the summaries in general orders have very few details.) Fragments of records from other sources, such as personal papers and looted regimental supply wagons, have made their way into the Museum of the Confederacy, the Gilder Lehrman Collection in New York City, and, rarely, into manuscript auctions. Other aspects of studying Confederate military justice records are found in *Confederate Death Sentences – A Reference Guide*, authored by Thomas P. Lowry and Lewis Laska, published 2008 by BookSurge. The following will clarify the citations for Confederate surgeons.

(anv0758) indicates microfilm frame 758 of National Archives microfilm M921, Roll One, "General Orders of the Army of Northern Virginia, August 11, 1861 to March 27, 1865."

Any citation with "mc" indicates a record held by the Museum of the Confederacy in Richmond, Virginia, thus "mc meiere" indicates the file of Dr. Meiere held by that institution. The museum staff is quite helpful in using the citations to access any given document.

Citations beginning with "glc" are in the Gilder Lehman Collection, thus "glc g.o. 22" indicates a document listed in their files as General Orders 22.

Other less frequent citations are "shsp" (The Southern Historical Society papers); "CMSR" (Compiled Military Service Record); and "rg109" (Record Group 109 at the National Archives).

Hope for future research into Confederate surgeons lies in the massive database being compiled by F. Terry Hambrecht, MD, who has been collecting information for years and plans publication of a *Magnum opus* in the not-too-distant future.

Appendix C

Dr. William G. Scott submitted a defense statement before his case went to the court-martial board for final decision. It will be recalled that he had allegedly stolen and sold a large quantity of government coffee. Here are his words verbatim:

"May it please your Honor and Gentlemen of the Commission. I would submit this case to your adjudication without a word in self vindication – fully assured in my own mind of the justice and character of the verdict, which the law and testimony warrants and which you will render without a moment's hesitation – But I cannot forego the favorable opportunity here presented of expressing my resentment and sense of the gross wrong and extreme injustice that has been done me by these malevolent and false aspersions upon the purity of my character and the freedom of my person.

"When the dread alarms of Civil Strife pealed her discordant knell along the banks of the Potomac and Treason marshaled her sanguinary hosts around the walls of our national metropolis, I heard and responded to the first call of my imperiled Country for succor – Abandoned a lucrative City practice – relinquished the ease and tranquility of home, and hastened to the incarnadined heights of Manassas and there among the rude conflict of arms – the shock of battle on that disastrous field jeopardized life liberty and all in giving to my bleeding Countrymen my humble but voluntary services. Again the wail of the wounded and dying soldiers broke upon my ear – my services were called and required in another and ruder quarter. Thither I hurried to obey my Country's call and over the rugged steeps and dangerous defiles of Western Virginia I followed the varying fortunes and shared the common dangers of our heroic little army through the wild waste and trackless forests of that inhospitable region – Hence I was called to the empurpled Plains of glorious old Shiloh and there amid the smoke and carnage of the raging battle on that blood-bought field re-baptized and consecrated anew my devotion to my Country and gave again my poor but gratuitous services to my suffering companions in arms. Called from hence to this city I was assigned the most arduous and disagreeable Hospital duties upon which I entered without hesitation or murmur upon the important and onerous tasks and I have the high assurance of my own Conscience and the testimony of those who served with me – that I discharged the delicate duties committed to my charge with honesty and fidelity – if not with skill and ability.

"After serving in this humble but laborious capacity for many months without adequate remuneration and discharging onerous and unpleasant labors to the entire satisfaction of all – I was suddenly arrested upon the base and unsupported allegations of some malevolent personal enemy and without inquiry into the guilt or innocence of my charge I was thrown into the loathsome vaults of gloomy and ignominious prison and there held in close confinement for the incredible and extraordinary space of three long months denied a copy of my charges and denied a speedy trial – the Birthright Constitutional Prerogative of every free American citizen.

"All this time my good name has been bandied about the streets. The commiseration and pity of the good and virtuous and the taunts and jeers of the evil disposed and wicked – the purlieus and sink vats of crime have been ransacked – the brothels and dens of vice and pollution have been searched and their low vile attainted inmates drawn forth to purchase my conviction. But even hardened vice and familiar sin halted and shrunk back appalled from the commission of a crime so monstrous.

"At last, after many importunities I have been brought to trial before this just and honorable Commission and what is the result of the examinations – And after a most thorough sifting and labored investigation, not one single scintilla of testimony has been developed to show the merest semblance of guilt much less to warrant a conviction and I shall here claim and demand an immediate and honorable acquittal. At your

Appendix C

hands, as the law directs and the facts should warrant – But, will this, sirs, repay the gross wrong, the foul injustice – will this requite the long weary hours of shame and contrition so casually inflicted & so unjustly endured? Will this restore my suffering name from the vile aspersions and unjust suspicions cast upon it by these false accusations and incarceration in a felons Bastille?

"Is this the price of my devotion to my Country? This the record of my disinterested labors in her service? Is it thus that she should repay the devotion and requite the perilous labors of those who heard and rallied to her first cry for succor? Who stood by her in tempest and storm when the weak despaired and the cold departed. Who pursued her fluctuations for time through 'good and evil report.' If such is to be the ungrateful return of all these services then you cannot too soon establish the fatal error, that the mischievous precedent may at once work out its evil ends, that man seek out elsewhere than in the Federal service for an asylum from outrage, violence, and wrong.

"You will pardon me, Gentlemen of the Commission, for expressing myself thus passionately, impressed as I am with the goading sense of foul wrong and deep injustice that has been so cruelly and wantonly done me. I thank you most sincerely for the candor and impartiality that have characterized your proceedings throughout these tedious and labored investigations.

"I have neither employed the ambidextrous dealings of the practiced jurist, nor have I indulged in the casuistry of the learned Metaphysicians and special pleaders – I leave the law and the evidence with you. I am no professional trixter [sic]. Even if I possessed the professional ability, the occasion does not call for its display. I shall submit the case to your discussion believing as I do that you will render an impartial and righteous verdict. And atone in part for the great wrong that has been done me by granting me an instant release from further duress and a full and honorable acquittal of the odious charges that that have been preferred against me – Gentleman the case is with you – I shall await your decision with no misgivings as to the character of the verdict which you will deem it your duty to render in accordance of the law and evidence in the case. God speed your decision. Let it be to the glory of justice and the honor of civilization."

In the format so favored by this generation's texters, these pages might be summarized as follows: NO STEAL THEY LIE.

Scott claimed combat surgery experience at Manassas and Shiloh, yet we discovered no records to substantiate such experience. As a final note, Scott claimed to have had a "lucrative City practice" before the Civil War. The 1860 census of the District of Columbia shows ten William Scotts. All were either laborers or tradesmen.

Index of Union Regiments

State Troops

Arkansas
1st Cavalry, 41
2nd Infantry, 6

California
4th Infantry, 48

Cherokee Nation
2nd Indian Brigade, 53

Colorado
1st Cavalry, 26

Connecticut
10th Infantry, 49
15th Infantry, 13
21st Infantry, 38, 60
27th Infantry, 29
Draft examiner, 56

Delaware
1st Cavalry, 58
3rd Infantry, 30

District of Columbia
Draft examiner, 34

Florida
1st Cavalry, 54

Illinois
5th Cavalry, 18, 67
7th Cavalry, 23
12th Cavalry, 29
13th Cavalry, 21
14th Infantry, 61
18th Infantry, 67
26th Infantry, 69
45th Infantry, 31
46th Infantry, 15
58th Infantry, 69
61st Infantry, 12
63rd Infantry, 26, 42
89th Infantry, 26
97th Infantry, 15
98th Infantry, 66
106th Infantry, 5
108th Infantry, 13
116th Infantry, 30
118th Infantry, 46
120th Infantry, 69
122nd Infantry, 57
124th Infantry, 33
148th Infantry, 59

Indiana
7th Cavalry, 4, 21
8th Cavalry, 67, 88
7th Infantry, 46
13th Infantry, 21
14th Infantry, 41
17th Infantry, 35
19th Infantry, 18
20th Infantry, 51
21st Infantry, 52
22nd Infantry, 58
40th Infantry, 51
43rd Infantry, 60
47th Infantry, 14
51st Infantry, 12
53rd Infantry, 54
57th Infantry, 43
58th Infantry, 1
63rd Infantry, 33
71st Infantry, 56
75th Infantry, 3

121

84th Infantry, 36
86th Infantry, 66
88th Infantry, 63
89th Infantry, 42
101st Infantry, 16

Iowa
   1st Cavalry, 56
   6th Infantry, 58
   27th Infantry, 27. 56
   35th Infantry, 12
   38th Infantry, 42
   40th Infantry, 53

Kansas
   2nd Cavalry, 54
   5th Cavalry, 31
   11th Cavalry, 1

Kentucky
   6th Cavalry, 35
   5th Infantry, 62
   8th Infantry, 53
   9th Infantry, 33
   20th Infantry, 46
   26th Infantry, 33
   34th Infantry, 63
   39th Infantry, 28
   54th Infantry, 42

Louisiana
   2nd Cavalry, 23

Maine
   1st Cavalry, 26
   5th Infantry, 67
   9th Infantry, 65
   15th Infantry, 16
   19th Infantry, 15
   20th Infantry, 4
   30th Veteran Volunteers, 10

Maryland
   1st Potomac Home Guard, 6
   2nd Veteran Volunteers, 4
   4th Infantry, 10
   5th Infantry, 23
   6th Infantry, 45
   7th Infantry, 6

Massachusetts
   4th Cavalry, 55
   12th Infantry, 1
   15th Infantry, 54
   18th Infantry, 30, 58
   19th Infantry, 36
   28th Infantry, 47, 60
   30th Infantry, 25
   31st Infantry, 36
   37th Infantry, 14, 43
   45th Infantry, 65
   54th Infantry, 7
   57th Infantry, 28

Michigan
   7th Cavalry, 66
   8th Cavalry, 65
   11th Infantry, 18, 48
   16th Infantry, 69
   24th Infantry, 65
   27th Infantry, 15

Minnesota
   2nd Cavalry, 66
   Independent Battery, 2
   1st Infantry, 51
   10th Infantry, 9

Missouri
   3rd Cavalry, 3
   8th Cavalry, MSM, 7
   10th Cavalry, 19
   11th Cavalry, 38

Index of Union Regiments

12th Cavalry, 46
2nd Artillery, 57
3rd Infantry, 37
4th Infantry, 6
6th Infantry, 34, 66
7th Infantry, 63
10th Infantry, 44
12th Infantry, 34
15th Infantry, 55
17th Infantry, 1, 41
21st Veteran Volunteers, 14
35th Infantry, 37

New Hampshire
   14th Infantry, 63

New Jersey
   6th Infantry, 13
   8th Infantry, 52
   12th Infantry, 23
   15th Infantry, 58
   22nd Infantry, 51
   23rd Infantry, 13
   26th Infantry, 64
   34th Infantry, 62

New York
   1st Cavalry Veteran Volunteers, 53
   2nd Cavalry, 65
   4th Cavalry, 21
   6th Cavalry, 56
   8th Cavalry, 22
   10th Cavalry, 58
   16th Cavalry, 17
   2nd Heavy Artillery, 2, 69
   5th Heavy Artillery, 16
   9th Heavy Artillery, 55
   14th Heavy Artillery, 50
   15th Heavy Artillery, 25
   16th Heavy Artillery, 48
   2nd Mounted Rifles, 69

3rd Infantry, 62
5th Veteran Volunteers, 53
5th Infantry, 66
6th Infantry, 49
7th Infantry, 18, 45, 52, 54
8th Infantry, 30, 38
11th Infantry, 24
13th Infantry, 37, 39
17th Infantry, 15
20th Infantry, 28
22nd Infantry, 32
25th Infantry, 47
33rd Infantry, 45
39th Infantry, 61, 69
41st Infantry, 56, 64
42nd Infantry, 48
44th Infantry, 19
45th Infantry, 56
52nd Infantry, 53, 67
58th Infantry, 61
59th Infantry, 17
62nd Infantry, 5
65th Infantry, 24
69th Infantry, 52, 60
72nd Infantry, 58
75th Infantry, 4, 81
76th Infantry, 37
79th Infantry, 42
81st Infantry, 8
90th Infantry, 36
93rd Nat. Guard, 67
95th Infantry, 40, 51
97th Infantry, 13, 30, 32, 39
101st Infantry, 14
104th Infantry, 55
106th Infantry, 21
110th Infantry, 40
119th Infantry, 29
124th Infantry, 40, 64
125th Infantry, 1
131st Infantry, 4, 8

136th Infantry, 30
137th Infantry, 26, 31
144th Infantry, 38
146th Infantry, 7
155th Infantry, 19
158th Infantry, 65
165th Infantry, 31
173rd Infantry, 3
176th Infantry, 61, 63
186th Infantry, 3, 10
Draft examiner, 35

North Carolina (Union)
3rd Infantry, 53

Ohio
3rd Cavalry, 57
9th Cavalry, 65
7th Infantry, 19
16th Infantry, 18
18th Infantry, 33
32nd Infantry, 8, 8, 25
35th Infantry, 23, 70
37th Infantry, 67
38th Infantry, 7
43rd Infantry, 4, 44
47th Infantry, 61
53rd Infantry, 5, 10
58th Infantry, 21, 57
59th Infantry, 78
62nd Infantry, 56
72nd Infantry, 23
73rd Infantry, 55
74th Infantry, 68
91st Infantry, 68
92nd Infantry, 58
99th Infantry, 62, 69
101st Infantry, 11
105th Infantry, 62

108th Infantry, 29
180th Infantry, 10

Oregon
1st Infantry, 10

Pennsylvania
3rd Cavalry, 29
5th Cavalry, 27, 48, 56
17th Cavalry, 44
5th Reserve, 16, 37
27th Infantry, 24
35th Infantry, 25
37th Infantry, 36
46th Infantry, 9
48th Infantry, 44
55th Infantry, 38
56th Infantry, 14
63rd Infantry, 47
67th Infantry, 3, 49
69th Infantry, 59
71st Infantry, 40
76th Infantry, 57
77th Infantry, 41
79th Infantry, 70
81st Infantry, 5, 22
87th Infantry, 41
88th Infantry, 43
91st Infantry, 64
99th Infantry, 62
101st Infantry, 55
102nd Infantry, 20
114th Infantry, 14
121st Infantry, 68
122nd Infantry, 9
123rd Infantry, 2
127th Infantry, 52, 53
128th Infantry, 9
129th Infantry, 40

Index of Union Regiments

133rd Infantry, 35
134th Infantry, 12
143rd Infantry, 22, 57
150th Infantry, 51
155th Infantry, 29
201st Infantry, 28
203rd Infantry, 61

Rhode Island
5th Heavy Artillery, 25

Tennessee
6th Cavalry, 68

Vermont
7th Infantry, 5

West Virginia
2nd Cavalry, 46
2nd Mounted Infantry, 43
6th Infantry, 55, 68
7th Infantry, 29

Wisconsin
1st Cavalry, 49
1st Infantry, 16
3rd Infantry, 69
5th Infantry, 10, 68
16th Veteran Volunteers, 27
19th Infantry, 16
20th Infantry, 31
23rd Infantry, 60
Draft Examiner, 31

Federal Troops

African American Troops
4th Colored Heavy Artillery, 64
6th Colored Heavy Artillery, 64
7th Colored Heavy Artillery, 35
8th Colored Heavy Artillery, 15
1st US Colored Troops, 14, 68
3rd US Colored Troops, 35
5th US Colored Troops, 2
7th US Colored Troops, 17
9th US Colored Troops, 47
14th US Colored Troops, 2
15th US Colored Troops, 70
22nd US Colored Troops, 50
23rd US Colored Troops, 50, 73
30th US Colored Troops, 32
31st US Colored Troops, 68
32nd US Colored Troops, 48, 68
33rd US Colored Troops, 14
35th US Colored Troops, 15
38th US Colored Troops, 84
46th US Colored Troops, 40, 48
48th US Colored Troops, 31
49th US Colored Troops, 23
53rd US Colored Troops, 68
58th US Colored Troops, 24
74th US Colored Troops, 22
76th US Colored Troops, 8
78th US Colored Troops, 47
84th US Colored Troops, 45
100th US Colored Troops, 39
111th US Colored Troops, 16
117th US Colored Troops, 51

Regular Army
17th US Infantry, 13

Index of Confederate Regiments

Alabama
    3rd Cavalry, 100
    9th Infantry, 99

Arkansas
    13th Infantry, 100

Florida
    5th Infantry, 99, 102

Georgia
    7th Infantry, 100
    21st Infantry, 100
    Phillips Legion, 101

Kentucky
    4th Cavalry, 89, 99

Louisiana
    Foot rifles, 100

Mississippi
    16th Infantry, 102

    18th Infantry, 101

Missouri
    1st Infantry, 100

North Carolina
    2nd Cavalry, 101
    6th Infantry, 101
    12th Infantry, 101
    17th Infantry, 99
    35th Infantry, 101
    52nd Infantry, 100
    55th Infantry, 101

Tennessee
    10th Infantry, 101

Virginia
    13th Infantry, 100
    28th Infantry, 101

Other
    Pages 99-102

Made in the USA
Monee, IL
14 July 2025